Discovery Guide to

Rajasthan

with Delhi and Agra

by Kim Naylor

MICHAEL HAAG

Other guides published by Michael Haag

Aegean and Mediterranean Turkey
Eastern Turkey and the Black Sea Coast
Greece
Delphi and the Sacred Way
Egypt
Cairo
Alexandria: A History and a Guide
Zimbabwe
West Africa
East Africa
Ethnic London

Please send for our complete list:
Michael Haag Limited
PO Box 369, London NW3 4ER
England

Discovery Guide to Rajasthan, first edition

Rajasthan city maps reproduced by kind permission of the Rajasthan Tourism Development Corporation

Cover design by Colin Elgie

Typeset in 10/12pt Palatino and printed in Great Britain at The Bath Press, Lower Bristol Road, Bath BA2 3BL

Published by Michael Haag Limited, PO Box 369, London NW3 4ER, England

ISBN 0 902743 49 X

CONTENTS

Note that in addition to the Practical Background chapter, practical information sections can be found at the end of each regional chapter.

ABOUT THIS GUIDE

In her people, culture and landscape, India possesses a variety, richness and beauty that is unsurpassed. Each of her regions has its own distinct character and Rajasthan, though a land of harsh desert and rugged hills in the northwest corner of the country, is India at her most regal and romantic.

Rajasthan—the name means 'the Land of Princes'—encompasses the former city states of the Hindu Rajput rulers. This was the gateway into India for invaders from the west, and the Rajputs fought stubbornly, defending their lands against a succession of armies. Finally they were subdued by the Mughal emperors, but their gallantry and their acts of heroism have been lauded in local folklore ever since. Rajasthan resounds with the echoes of the Rajput's warring history, and everywhere there are formidable battle-scarred forts crowning craggy hilltops. But there is more than just a ghostly past.

A land larger than France, strewn with castles, intricately carved temples and fabulous palaces. Men wearing scarlet turbans and brightly dressed women laden with heavy jewellery. Bazaars piled with spices, pungent aromatics, silver, gold, silks and scores of local crafts. Huge camel and cattle fairs attended by over 100,000 people. Colourful religious festivals celebrated with an intensity unknown in the Western world. Steam trains cutting their paths across the desert wastes. Local bards roaming from village to village eulogising the ancient Rajput heroes. Tigers stalking the forests. Luxury hotels, once the palaces of maharajas, where guests are pampered like royalty. These are images of Rajasthan, an exotic corner of the Orient.

This Guide begins with a *Historical Background* chapter which will help put the places you visit in context. This is followed by a *Practical Background* chapter which explains how to travel within Rajasthan, with details on accommodation, money, planes, buses, trains, etc. And then subsequent chapters conduct you around Rajasthan, each chapter covering a city or region, pointing out what to see and supplying further on-the-spot historical and cultural background. Also, each chapter concludes with a *Practical Information* section listing a range of places to stay, from cheapest to most luxurious, plus other pertinent information.

To help with the next edition of this Guide, the reader is asked to send information and comments to the *General Editor, Discovery Guide to Rajasthan, Michael Haag Limited, PO Box 369, London NW3 4ER, England*. Thank you.

HISTORICAL BACKGROUND

Geography

To understand the people and history of Rajasthan, it is important to appreciate its geography.

Two distinct geographical features dominate Rajasthan: mountains and desert.

Mountains

The Aravalli Mountains, the highest mountains between the Himalayas and the Nilgiri Hills of southern India, stretch across Rajasthan from northeast to southwest. Indeed their very name means 'a shaft lying across'. The range starts modestly at Delhi, gradually building up to impressive looking peaks around Alwar, before dipping into a wide valley between Jaipur and Ajmer, ascending again to reach its densest and most rugged in the southern part of the state, culminating with its highest point at Mount Abu (1722 metres)—the 'Son of the Himalayas' according to the myths—which is on the border of Gujarat.

To the east of the Aravallis the undulating lands are green, forested and relatively fertile and in these hills and valleys the Chauhan, Sisodia and Kuchwaha Rajput clans and the Jat tribes carved out their kingdoms, building capitals at Chittorgarh, Ajmer, Amber, Udaipur, Alwar, Kotah, Bundi and Bharatpur. To the west of the Aravallis unfolds the vast flat arid expanse of the Thar Desert.

Desert

The Thar or Great Indian Desert is a section of the span of desert which sweeps the world from the Sahara, across Arabia, through Rajasthan and finally ending in Central Asia as the Gobi Desert. The Bhatti and Rathore clans laid claim to vast tracts of the empty and barren Thar and out of the sand they built for themselves imposing citadels at Jaisalmer, Jodhpur and Bikaner.

Various rivers—notably the Chambal, the Banas, the Berach, the Kotari, the Khari, the Morel, the Kali Sindh and the Banganga—cut their paths through eastern Rajasthan providing life to a rich fauna and flora. But in the Thar, a region periodically afflicted by drought, only the River Luni (and her tributaries), rising at Pushkar and flowing through the southwestern part of the state into the Rann of Kutch offers a lifeline to the desert people. Elsewhere wells and small lakes serve as oases and in the northwest of the state the remarkable Rajasthan Canal, running parallel with the Pakistan border from Haryana State to the town of Ramgarh northwest of Jaisalmer, provides water for irrigation and consumption.

Invasion route

Rajasthan's very location exposed it to the influences of invasions and migrations entering into northwest India. As guardians at the gateway the Rajputs fought off the outside world, though at times they absorbed aspects of it. Furthermore the geography of Rajasthan itself meant that fertile lands were extremely precious, especially as the clans grew and their kingdoms were divided amongst an ever increasing number of sons, and the Rajput families were constantly fighting between themselves. Fate of birth—the Rajputs are born of the martial caste—and of geography, moulded the Rajputs' character and their history.

The Rajput Character

Code of honour

As noble warriors, honour was fundamental to the Rajput ethos. During their most heroic medieval period they would prefer to die in battle rather than forsake their honour through submission. When defeat on the battlefield looked imminent, the men would don their saffron robes—the garb worn only for their weddings and ritual martyrdom—and fight to the death while their women, dressed in their bridal clothes, would commit johar by climbing a blazing pyre and immolating themselves.

In victory the Rajput was magnanimous, often setting his prisoners free or not even bothering to pursue his defeated foe. Such generosity was rather reckless and there were occasions when the enemy recuperated and returned to fight again—the most devastating example was Mohammed Ghori, who

Lovers by a lotus pool, c1700

came back to slaughter Prithviraj Chauhan at the second Battle of Tarain in 1192.

In the 16th C some of the Rajput clans, such as the Kuchwahas, contravened their strict codes by marrying into the ruling Mughal dynasty and by doing so they secured for themselves a life of comfort and prosperity. Those families, like the Sisodias, who scorned such alliances and upheld their independence and honour suffered by sinking into relative obscurity.

Passionate living

In his private life the Rajput was hard living. He hunted, loved passionately, ate meat, drank wine and consumed afion (opium). James Tod noted: 'The Bhatti is to the full as addicted as any of his brethren to the immoderate use of opium. To the umlpani, or "infusion", succeeds the pipe, and they continue inhaling mechanically the smoke long after they are insensible to all that is passing around them; nay, it is said, you may scratch or pinch them while in this condition without exciting sensation. The hooka is the dessert of the umlpani; the panacea for all the ills which can overtake the Rajpoot, and with which he can at any time enjoy a paradise of his own creation. To ask a Bhatti for a whiff of his pipe would be deemed a direct insult'.

Female infanticide was commonly practised, but as Tod observed, 'In medieval Europe convents and nunneries were filled by unwanted, dowerless daughters of the feudal nobility. The Rajput preferred to end the sad life before it had begun'. If the female survived this first whittling down ritual

Women's role

she too was then subject to a life of rigid etiquette. She was married off at a young age to a man of her father's choice: usually there were political motives behind the marriage and the union was made to establish a bond between two families. A woman was often expected to respect strict purdah from the age of puberty until death (purdah is still practised in the remoter and more traditional regions of Rajasthan), and so she was confined to the women's quarters of the household for most of her life. When her husband died she climbed his funeral pyre to perform sati, the ultimate sacrifice to her master. Sati hands imprinted on fort walls are a vivid reminder of the dedication expected of a woman. And then in battle they burnt themselves to death en masse before their husbands went out to their own ritual suicide.

In stark contrast to the Rajputs' brutal life on the battlefield was their lavish and luxurious life in their fabulous palaces. The Rajputs were great patrons and lovers of the arts and this you will quickly appreciate when you visit the former royal households and the museums which are scattered around Rajasthan.

Other Peoples of Rajasthan

India has an enormous variety of peoples—there is a kaleidoscope of ethnic groups around the country, each observing its own religion and praying to its favourite deities. In addition, the lores of ancient traditions have imposed on communities the rigid social stratification of the caste system. Rajasthan is a microcosm of this world, with its own multitude of different peoples. The Rajputs—Hindus from the princely and warrior caste of kshatriyas—is just one group, which in turn is divided into numerous sub-groups. Below is a brief summary of some of the other people you will encounter during travels in Rajasthan.

Banjaras: An itinerant class of trader and artisan, the Banjaras are drawn from various castes. Traditionally they used to transport salt from Rajasthan to markets around north India and they would also carry the provisions for armies on the move.

Bhats and Charans: Traditionally the Bhats were the bards, heralds and court poets, while the Charans, who shared a close bond with the Rajputs, were the itinerant minstrels.

Bhils: The aboriginal Bhils are the oldest inhabitants of Rajasthan and once they dominated much of this area. Early invaders pushed the Bhils aside and it is probably they who initiated the legend about the Bhils' origins: 'A beautiful damsel passed through the spot where Lord Mahadeva was in agony from fever. The sight of the girl relieved Mahadeva of his suffering and later he married her. She gave birth to seven male children. One of them was ugly. Mahadeva could not bear the sight of him and banished him. It is said all the Bhils are his descendants' (from a history written by a local authority). More pleasing are the tales about the Bhils' courage on the battlefield—they were expert archers—and how they fought alongside the Rajputs in defence of Mewar. Today they tend to live in their own communities, farming small plots. And, despite slowly getting absorbed into the mainstream, they still maintain many of their colourful and rather curious customs. These, judging from the amount of literature written about the Bhils, are of great interest to ethnographers.

Brahmins: Priests by tradition and hence custodians of the Hindu culture, the Brahmins are top of the social hierarchy. Though in real terms, or rather as far as landownership or material wealth is concerned, they do not necessarily command poll position. Nowadays Brahmins are also involved in agriculture, the services and trade.

Gadia Lohars: Also nomadic are the Gadia Lohars, Rajasthan's colourful gypsies, who wander from village to village in their bullock carts offering their services as blacksmiths. Theirs is a dying trade, and now that the Gadia Lohars are falling on hard times local governments are trying to settle them.

Girasias: Also of ancient descent are the Girasias who are farmers and similar to the Bhils. They are from the Mewar region and apparently descendants from a marriage between Rajputs and Bhils.

Gujars: These are the cattle breeders and cultivators commonly found in the eastern regions of Rajasthan around Bharatpur and Alwar.

Jats: The most prominent agriculturists in Rajasthan are the Jats, similar to the Gujars. Hard working and sturdy in their build, they are particularly dominant in the Bikaner and Jodhpur regions and in the past they were the rajas of Bharatpur. The Jats are divided into two main sects: the Jasnathi was founded by Jasnath in AD 1488 and its members wear a black cord around their neck; the Bishnois, the other sect, follow 29 principles which were laid down by their guru Jambaji—hence their name Bees (twenty) Nau (nine)—and these include abstaining from wine, tobacco and the killing of animals. Unlike most Hindus, these two sects bury their dead rather than burn them.

Kathodis: The 'Katha' is a gatherer living a nomadic life in southern Mewar. It seems that theirs is a desperate lot, for after the harvest they are out of work until the next season. Today, though, the Kathodi is being given land on which to cultivate his own crops.

Meenas: One of the oldest of the indigenous peoples are the Meenas who once ruled tracts of northeast Rajasthan, including Amber until they were ousted by the Kuchwahas. Meenas are divided into two groups, the Zamindari, who are well to do farmers, and the Chowkidari, who guard the villages, though in the past they were infamous for their pilfering.

Rebaris: The Rebaris claim that they descend from a union between the Rajputs and the Apsaras—the heavenly damsels. They are semi-nomadic camel breeders wandering around the northern part of west Rajasthan and they are well known for their intimate knowledge of this region—indeed, their name is derived from 'Rebar' meaning 'a guide' in Persian.

Sahariyas: 'Wild men' as the Sahariyas are known are a community living around Kotah district who, apparently, fell foul of their debts somewhere along the line and became victims of the money lenders. Local government is trying to alleviate their position by rescuing them from their past.

Sansis: A locally written ethnographic study has the following to say about the Sansis: 'The Sansis are nomadic people, notoriously known for their criminal habits . . . These tribal people are averse to settlement. They live in impoverished shanties on the outskirts of towns and villages, which provide them with convenient bases of operation . . . During the celebrations of marriage, alcoholic drinks flow like water. All guests, both men and women, drink and dance till midnight and sex taboos are forgotten . . . After the ceremony the couples retire to their own room and the next morning, the groom has to declare publicly that the bride was found to be an absolute virgin'.

Vaisyas: As the mercantile class the Vaisyas are well known for their business acumen. And particularly astute are the Marwaris—or Mahajans—from the Shekavati region. The many groups of Vaisyas include the Agarwals, Khandelwals, Oswals, Maheshwaris, Saraogis and Porwals. These groups are divided further—the Oswals alone, for example, have 2000 sub-groups.

Lieutenant-Colonel James Tod

James Tod, born in 1782, joined the East India Company's army corps as a cadet in 1798 and rose to become the British Political Agent for the Western Rajput States before quitting his service in 1822.

Chronicler of Rajputana

During his career Tod developed a great admiration for the Rajputs and amassed a huge amount of information about this illustrious warrior caste, their history and their lands. Indeed his undisguised respect for the Rajputs may well have been the cause of his premature 'retirement'. Bishop Heber wrote in 1824: 'His misfortune was that, in consequence of his favouring the native princes so much, the Government of Calcutta [the British] were led to suspect him of corruption, and consequently to narrow his powers and associate other officers with him in his trust till he was disgusted and resigned his place. They are now, I believe, well satisfied that their suspicions were groundless. Captain Tod is strenuously vindicated from the charge by all the officers with whom I have conversed, and some of whom had abundant means of knowing what the natives themselves thought of him'.

On returning to England Tod fastidiously compiled his material into two detailed volumes entitled the *Annals and Antiquities of Rajasthan* which were published in 1829–32. His tomes—an encyclopedia of Rajputana—painstakingly document the rise and fall of the Rajput clans and recount numerous colourful tales illustrating the chivalry, reckless courage, passion and code of honour of these romantic medieval knights.

Tod scoured the hills and deserts of Rajputana to research his book and many of his sources were heroic poems composed by local bards and tales related by opium eaters. (Rajputs were addicted to opium and even today it is commonly consumed in the villages of Rajasthan.) So there are fabulous stories of glorification, but Tod's is a serious work with much accurate information and it remains the best and most definitive account of the peoples and lands of Rajasthan yet to be published.

History

The Rajputs' obscure and confused racial origins have been debated at great length, but still there is no definitive conclusion about where they came from. The Rajputs themselves claim they are of Aryan stock and are descendants of the kshatriyas,

The Rajputs: Hindu warriors

the Hindus' martial caste, who were called upon to defend India during the ancient Brahmana (late Vedic) period between 900 and 500 BC. They believe their ancestors were born of the mythological Suryavansh (Solar), Chandravansh (Lunar) and Agnivansh (Fire) races which traced their origins back to Rama—incarnations of Vishnu, Krishna and the agnikund (fire pit) at Mount Abu respectively.

The three races were sub-divided into 36 Rajput clans which gradually emerged and carved territories for themselves. The most important of the Suryavansh clans were the Guhilots or Sisodias of Mewar (Chittorgarh and Udaipur), the Rathores of

ERSTWHILE STATES OF RAJPUTANA

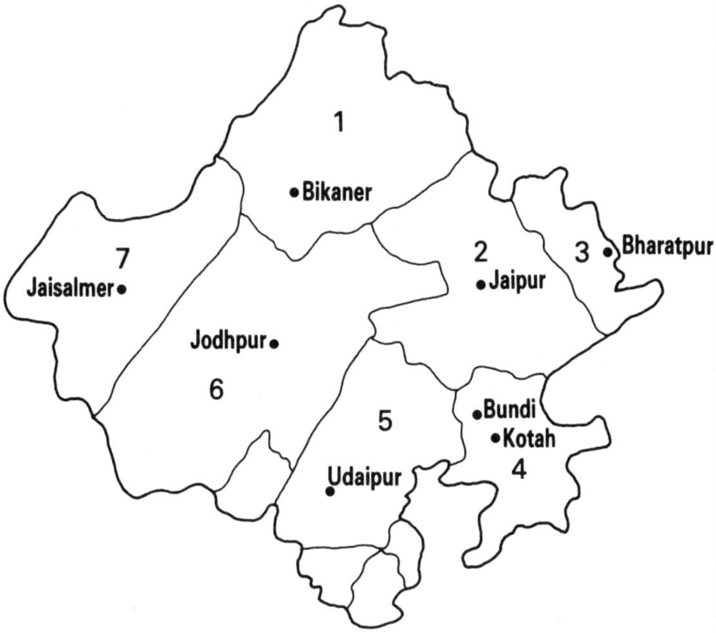

1. Rathores of Bikaner
2. Kuchwahas of Jaipur
3. Jats of Bharatpur
4. Harachauhans of Bundi and Kotah
5. Sisodias of Mewar
6. Rathores of Marwar
7. Bhattis of Jaisalmer

Marwar and the splinter group of Bikaner (Jodhpur and Bikaner) and the Kuchwahas of Dhundar (Amber and Jaipur). Of the Chandravansh the Bhattis of Jaisalmer were the most significant. And created from the sacred agnikund at Mount Abu by the sage Vashist were the Chauhans of Ajmer and Delhi with their clan branches at Sirohi and, later, Haravati (Bundi and Kotah).

Suffice to say that in the 8th C AD, when the Arabs conquered Sindh and were launching raids into

India, the Gurjara-Pratiharas dynasty—acknowledged as forefathers of the Rajput clans—were guardians of the northwestern gateway into the sub-continent.

Early in the 11th C Mahmud of Ghazni controlled a vast area of central Asia and from his capital at Ghazni, south of present Kabul, he overran Punjab and plundered cities as far east as Varanasi. But it was not until the end of the 12th C that India and the Rajputs—now evolved into their clans and prepared to defend their homelands and uphold Hinduism—experienced their first full-scale Moslem invasion.

Moslem invasion

In 1191 the Turko-Afghan Mohammed Ghori marched into India and attacked Delhi, but he and his army of 200,000 cavalry and 3000 elephants were repulsed by Prithviraj Chauhan. Internal feuding divided and weakened the Rajputs (the Chauhans and the Rathores were bitter rivals) and they also underestimated the tenacity of their Moslem aggressors. When Ghori returned the following year he defeated Prithviraj at the Battle of Tarain, took Ajmer and routed the Rathores. Qutb-ud-din, his general, captured Delhi in 1193 and, after Ghori's death in 1206, he became the first Sultan of Delhi. Thus commenced the Sultanate of Delhi and Moslem rule in northern India.

Late in the 13th C Alaudin Khilji extended the sultanate's sway into Rajputana after he defeated heroic Rajput opposition at Ranthambore and Chittorgarh. The Rajputs proved to be remarkably resilient and they fought passionately, preferring to die in battle than submit to the enemy.

Infighting amongst Moslem factions at Delhi, Malwa and Gujarat in the 16th C heralded the opportunity for the Rajputs to regain lost territories. Rana Sanga, the Sisodia chief and most able soldier of the day, expanded his Mewar kingdom, defeated the forces of Sultan Ibrahim Lodi of Delhi on two occasions and called upon fellow Rajputs to unite and oust the Moslems once and for all.

But an effete Delhi sultanate was also a signal

to would-be invaders from abroad that the time for attack was ripe. In 1523 Barbur, a descendant of Tamerlane (Timor) of Samarkand, marched into India from his capital at Kabul. He triumphed against the Sultan of Delhi at the Battle of Panipat—despite being outnumbered four to one—and went on to establish his own dynasty, the Mughals, which was to have a profound and everlasting effect on India.

The Mughals

After his victory Barbur had to contend with the Rajput confederacy, led by Rana Sanga, who were also vying for supremacy in northern India. In 1527 the two armies met at Kanuha, near Bharatpur, where the Rajputs lost. This tragic defeat put a sudden end to the Rajput resurgence and aspirations for a great empire of their own. Nevertheless they, or at least some of their clans, were to become some of the sharpest thorns in the Mughals' flesh over the following generations.

Having immobilised the Rajputs, Barbur concentrated on extending his territories along the plains of northern India. On his death in 1530 he was succeeded by his son Humayun, who proved unable to consolidate the empire and was usurped by Sher Shah, an Afghan chief, ten years later.

Meanwhile in Rajputana the gallant Sisodias had faded somewhat into the background, licking their wounds after suffering serious defeats on the battlefield. At this time Maldeo, leader of the Rathores, rose as the prominent Rajput and won back Ajmer and even put Sher Shah's soldiers to flight when they attacked his kingdom of Marwar.

Humayun returned from exile in 1555 to win back his throne at Delhi from Sher Shah's inept successors, but he died the following year thus allowing power to fall to his teenage son Akbar, who turned out to be the most brilliant of the great Mughal emperors.

Any dreams Maldeo and the Rajputs may have had for toppling the Mughals were dashed early in Akbar's reign. The young emperor turned his attention to Rajputana, winning back Ajmer from

Maldeo and finally forcing the worthy Rathore into accepting his rule.

However, Akbar—an enlightened man who embraced all religions without prejudice—had a far more effective tactic than the sword. He married into the Rajput clans and by bringing them into his Mughal fold he was able to rely on them as allies with varying degrees of success. In 1561 the Kuchwahas of Amber set the precedent when Raja Bharmal gave his daughter in marriage to Akbar. Their son, Salim, later became Emperor Jahangir. Quite typically the Rajput clans squabbled amongst themselves and some looked to Akbar as a possible source of support to help them in their internal feuds. Indeed, it is believed that Bharmal allied himself with the emperor so as to deter rivals within his own household. The Kuchwahas had feathered their own bed and, though vassals to the emperor, their loyalty to the Mughals ensured their security and rise to prosperity.

Defiance by the Sisodias of Mewar

Akbar faced a different sort of character when he confronted the Sisodias of Mewar. Colonel Tod, celebrated documenter of the Rajputs, commented: 'Mewar alone, the sacred bulwark of religion, never compromised her honour for her safety . . . The blood of her princes has flowed in copious streams for the maintenance of this honour, religion, and independence'. After an historic and horrific battle, Chittorgarh, the capital of Mewar, fell on 25 February 1568. The following year Akbar received submission from the Haras at Ranthambore castle.

Akbar tried peaceful methods to entice the Sisodias to accept Mughal supremacy, but with no luck. The Rajputs of Mewar chose to uphold honour and wage their idealistic though foolhardy war against the stronger emperor. Under their charismatic Rana Pratap they fought and lost their most celebrated Battle of Haldighati in 1576.

Pratap escaped into the Aravalli hills where he slowly regathered his forces. Meanwhile Akbar had consolidated his influence in Rajputana by cultivating friendships with the clans, and the Rathores of Marwar and of Bikaner and the Bhattis of Jaisalmer had all realised it was easier and far more profitable to accept Mughal domination than to fight it. By the end of the 16th C Akbar had all of Rajputana under his control except stubborn pockets of Mewar.

Though their defiance of the Mughals was admirable the Sisodias were the losers. While the other Rajput rulers held prominent positions in the Mughal court and still retained a degree of autonomy and dignity, despite being vassals, the rana grew obscure and impoverished. When the Sisodias did finally conclude a quasi peace with Jahangir they were exempted from ever sending their king to pay homage at the imperial court, a unique privilege enjoyed by no other Rajput clan. But by now, the 17th C, Mewar was no longer the pre-eminent Rajput principality, rather this position was held by the flourishing states of Amber and Marwar.

Jahangir was succeeded by his son Shah Jahan, who in turn was ousted and imprisoned by his son Aurangzeb in 1658. Emperor Aurangzeb, a Moslem zealot, reimposed the jiziya—the old tax enforced on non-Moslems which had been banned by Akbar—and antagonised Hindus with his religious bigotry. The Rathores rebelled and for a while some of the Rajput clans united against the Mughals.

Decline of the Mughal empire

With the death of Aurangzeb—the last of the six 'Great Mughals'—in 1707, the Mughal empire began to crumble. Though the Mughals had limited the Rajputs' independence during the last 150 years they had, nevertheless, introduced cosmopolitanism into the Rajputs' otherwise insular culture. Sawai Jai Singh of Amber and Jaipur is a fine example of a ruler who took advantage of this contact with the outer world and, indeed, throughout Rajputana art and scholarship at all levels benefited from Mughal influence.

Even more significant was that as superior overlords the Mughals managed to provide relative stability in Rajputana, a fact only too apparent when their control began to wane and the Rajput clans

Maharana Bhim Singh, ruler of Mewar (1778–1828), during Rajputana's period of hedonistic decline

reverted to fighting amongst themselves. At the same time the Marathas, who rose up from central India to chip away the decaying Mughal empire, also challenged the Rajputs. The result was anarchy and disaster and in the words of Tod, the 'total ruin and humiliation of this noble (Rajput) race'.

Anarchy in Rajputana

In 1739 the Persian Nadir Shah sacked Delhi and carried off the Peacock Throne; the rapidly declining Mughal empire finally drew to an end with the death of Bahadur Shah II in 1862. The Marathas' ambitions were suddenly cut short in 1761 when they were decisively trounced on the battlefield of Panipat by Ahmed Shah Durani from Afghanistan. By now the British, already well entrenched in India, were expanding their influence and were later to create their own empire there.

The British

In the 19th C the various Rajput princely states signed treaties with the British in return for protection; the Rajputs' illustrious days of fighting for honour and independence on the battlefield were something of the past and best remembered in folk tales. When India gained her independence from the British in 1947 Rajputana consented to join the Indian Union and later became the State of Rajasthan, the third largest state in the Indian Republic. The erstwhile rulers, like the other maharajas around India, received privy purses in return for their loss of territories, but even this was abolished by Prime Minister Indira Gandhi in 1970.

Suddenly in need of income many of the old royal families opened up their historic homes to the public. Today their fabulous ancestral palaces and forts —monuments from India's most romantic and colourful eras—have been splendidly converted into museums and hotels and are amongst the country's finest and best loved tourist attractions.

Historical Chronology

2500–1500 BC	The Harappan culture in the Indus valley.
1500	Aryan invasion destroys Indus valley civilisation and enters north India.

1500–900	Composition of the Rig Veda Hymns.
900	The Mahabharata War.
900–500	Brahmana Period.
566–486	Gautama Buddha.
528	Death of Mahavira, founder of Jainism.
327	Alexander the Great invades northwest India.
322–183	**Mauryan Period.**
322–298	Chandragupta.
269–232	Ashoka.
190 BC– AD 350	Various waves of invaders push into northwest India.
320–540	**Gupta Period,** founded by Chandragupta I.
454	Huns—possible ancestors of the Rajputs—invade India.
606–647	**Harsha Period.**
622	Birth of Islam.
712	Arabs occupy Sindh.
750–1019	Gurjara–Pratihara period.
1018	Mahmud of Ghazni sacks Kanauj and plunders Hindu states.
1192	Second Battle of Tarain, victory for Mohammed Ghori against Prithviraj Chauhan.
1206–1526	**Sultanate of Delhi.**
1296–1316	Alaudin Khilji.
1325–1351	Mohammed ibn Tughlak.
1498	Vasco da Gama reaches India.
1526	Battle of Panipat. Barbur defeats Sultan Ibrahim Lodi.
1526–1862	**Mughal Dynasty.**
1526–1530	Barbur.
1527	Battle of Kanuha, Barbur defeats Rajput confederacy.
1530–1556	Humayun. Sher Shah usurps the Mughal throne at Delhi in 1540; Humayun retakes it in 1555.
1556–1605	Akbar.

1561	Akbar marries Rajput princess.
1568	Akbar lays siege to Chittorgarh.
1576	Battle of Haldigathi. Defeat of Rana Pratap of Mewar.
1605–1627	Jahangir.
1612	British establish their first trading post at Surat.
1616	Sir Thomas Roe meets Jahangir in Ajmer; this was the first official British-Mughal contact.
1627–1658	Shah Jahan.
1631	Work begins on the Taj Mahal, the tomb of Shah Jahan's wife Mumtaz Mahal.
1658–1707	Aurangzeb; Shah Jahan dies in prison in 1666.
Late 17th C	Rise of the Marathas of central India under Shivaji.
1739	Persians plunder the Mughals' Peacock Throne.
1757	Battle of Plassey. British defeat the French in India, a major step towards establishing their own empire in India.
1818	British defeat the Marathas and become effective rulers of India.
1857	Indian Mutiny. The British government takes over the rule of India from the East India Company.
1862	Bahadur Shah II, the last of the Mughals, dies in exile.
1877	Queen Victoria proclaimed Empress of India. The British Empire in India is at its height.
Early 20th C	Nationalist movement in India largely inspired by Mahatma Gandhi.
1947	India gains her independence from the British, but divides into two countries, India and Pakistan.
1948	Mahatma Gandhi assassinated at Delhi.

The Protagonists

The Rajputs (in chronological order)

Jaisal: The Bhatti king who founded Jaisalmer in 1156.

Prithviraj Chauhan: The great Chauhan king and warrior who operated from Ajmer. He repulsed Mohammed Ghori at the first Battle of Tarain in 1191, but allowed his defeated enemy freedom. Ghori returned the following year to overcome Prithviraj at the second Battle of Tarain. In local legends Prithviraj is portrayed as a dashing prince charming and many a princess gave him the glad eye. A romance between him and the daughter of Jaichand, the powerful rival ruler of Kanauj, was part of the reason for the continued fighting between the two kings, which left the lands disunited and vulnerable to invasion.

The beautiful Padmini

Padmini: The Sisodia queen whose beauty so infatuated Alaudin that he connived to win her for his harem. When his attempt failed, Alaudin laid siege to Chittorgarh (1302 and the result was the first of the Sisodia's horrific johars in which Padmini honourably mounted the funeral pyre. Her tragic tale is one of the most famous in Rajasthani folklore.

Rana Kumbha: The distinguished 15th C Sisodia king who frequently fought off the Moslem sultans and who is also famous as a prolific builder of forts, temples and other monuments and as a writer and patron of the arts.

Jodha: The Rathore king who founded Jodhpur in 1459.

Bika: Son of Jodha who in the late 15th C created his own Rathore kingdom in north Rajputana with its capital at Bikaner.

Rana Sanga: One of the great heroes in the Sisodia's hall of fame. Rana Sanga's role was pivotal in the history of Rajputana and indeed India. Under Sanga the Rajputs united—for once—to oppose Barbur's invasion. They lost the Battle of Kanuha in 1527—the Rajputs claim Barbur won unfairly

Defeat at the hands of the Mughals

because 'he did not play the battle according to the moral rules of the game'—and this heralded the start of the Mughal empire in India.

Maldeo: The Rathore king who ruled between 1532 and 1562 and was behind Marwar's rise to preeminence amongst the Rajput clans during this period.

Udai Singh: The Sisodia king who founded Udaipur in 1568.

Man Singh: The very able though notably modest Kuchwaha king, politician and soldier. He was an early victim of the Akbar-Kuchwaha alliance: as a senior general in Akbar's army he was pitched against fellow Rajputs, the most famous occasion being Haldighati (1576) when he fought the great Rana Pratap.

Rana Pratap: The most revered of all the Rajput heroes and symbol of courage, patriotism and integrity. Pratap's greatest battle was Haldighati in 1576 against Akbar's army under the command of Man Singh. Pratap lost, but he never succumbed to Akbar; there is an old saying: 'Akbar collected many rulers like stones, but a jewel like Pratap always eluded him'.

Mizra Jai Singh: Another Kuchwaha king who proved to be a fine 'all-rounder'. While a scholar and great patron of the arts, Mizra Jai Singh, who ruled from 1617–67, was supportive of the Mughals on the battlefield and in politics. He finally fell out with Aurangzeb, who, it was rumoured, had him poisoned.

Jaswant Singh: The charismatic 17th C Rathore ruler of Marwar, who, though in the service of Mughals, stood up against Aurangzeb's oppressive Islamic dogmas. Jaswant died in obscurity in Afghanistan, his dreams of ridding Rajputana of Aurangzeb's authority unfulfilled.

The brilliant founder of Jaipur

Sawai Jai Singh: The highly talented and versatile Kuchwaha ruler, who, not a soldier in the classic Rajput mould, was nevertheless an exceptional statesman. During his long reign (1700–43) he became an authority on astronomy, science and the arts and was universally respected for his erudition.

Maharaja Sawai Jai Singh, the founder of Jaipur

He founded the splendid city of Jaipur and moved his capital there from Amber. Since its creation Jaipur has been the foremost city in Rajasthan.

Durga Das: The inspired and heroic Rathore freedom fighter who fought stubbornly against Aurangzeb. One of his prime objectives was to help enthrone Ajit, posthumous son of Jaswant Singh, on the Jodhpur gaadi, which he finally succeeded in doing in 1709.

Ganga Singh: An enlightened 20th C maharaja of Bikaner. Ganga Singh did much to improve the conditions of his state by making use of modern technology. In return he received universal respect and remains even after his death something of a father figure to the people of Bikaner.

The Moslems (in chronological order)

Mahmud of Ghazni: Second in line of the Afghan Ghazni dynasty. Mahmud who reigned from 997 to 1030, extended the family empire into northwest India and in 1018 he seized Kanauj. His wave of Moslems was the first to invade India and those who followed his example over the next 500 years did so with increasing determination and success.

Mohammed Ghori: The leader of the Afghan Ghori dynasty who ousted Mahmud of Ghazni's weak successors and revived the colonisation of northwest India. At his second attempt in 1192 Ghori defeated Prithviraj Chauhan at Tarain—'For miles the stricken field was bestrewn with castaway flags and spears and shields, and heaped bows, jewelled swords and plumed casques, exquisitely chiselled and damascened gauntlets, breast-plates and gaily-dyed scarves, intermingled with countless dead'—and his armies continued eastwards conquering almost all that lay in their path as far as the Bay of Bengal.

First sultan of Delhi

Qutb-ud-din Aibak: An ex-slave and Mohammed Ghori's general who succeeded Mohammed after his assassination in 1206 and adopted the title Sultan of Delhi.

Alaudin Khilji: A tough ruler who imposed draconian laws on his subjects and who had murdered his uncle in 1296 to gain the Delhi Sultanate. He extended his territories far southwards. In Rajasthan he is famous for his attack on Chittorgarh in 1302 and his fateful dalliance with the beautiful Padmini.

Muhammad Tughluk: Second in line of the Tughluk dynasty in Delhi who assumed power in 1325. He was an able ruler, though rather eccentric—the traveller Ibn Batuta wrote: 'Muhammad above all men delights most in giving presents and shedding blood. At his door is seen always some pauper on the way to wealth or some corpse that has been executed'.

Timor (Tamerlane): The warrior from Samarkand who conquered a huge Asian empire and invaded India in 1398. Timor destroyed Delhi and left, doing nothing to repair his damage.

Ibrahim Lodi: One of the Lodi dynasty which gained control of Delhi in the latter half of the 15th C and provided the city once again with some sort of stability. Ibrahim came to the throne in 1517, but his rivals called upon the support of Barbur who, having consolidated his power to the west in Samarkand and Afghanistan, was champing for new conquests. At the ensuing Battle of Panipat in 1526, Barbur defeated and killed Ibrahim.

The Mughals (in chronological order)

Barbur: A direct descendant of Timor and Genghis Khan and the founder of the Mughal dynasty in India after his success at the Battle of Panipat in 1526. 'Hindustan is a country which has few pleasures to recommend it', was Barbur's verdict after he had had a chance to look around, but he was impressed by the monsoon rains and the abundance of gold and silver. In 1527 he defeated the Rajput confederacy under Rana Sanga at Khanua and that more or less extinguished the Hindus' hopes of restoring their supremacy in northern India. Barbur died in 1530.

Humayun: Barbur's son and successor, Humayun

proved his ability with early victories against his opponents, but then his complacency allowed him to lapse into laziness and Sher Khan (later renamed Sher Shah) managed to usurp the Mughal throne in 1540. Humayun fled to Rajputana but he returned from exile in 1555, ten years after Sher Shah's death, to win back Delhi; he died the following year.

Sher Shah: The Afghan governor of Bihar who extended his territories to Bengal and went on to overcome Humayun. He was a remarkable ruler, expanding the Mughal empire and establishing excellent administrative order. Sher Shah died in 1545 and was followed by two inept successors before Humayun retrieved his throne in 1555.

The greatest Mughal prince

Akbar: The son of Humayun, the greatest of the Mughals and one of the finest rulers in India's history. Akbar inherited his throne in 1556 at the age of 13. He increased the empire and he had the enlightened proclivity to embrace all religions and philosophies. In Rajputana he set a precedent by establishing treaties with the kings, often cementing the bond by marrying one of his own family with a prince or princess of the Rajput clan. Or he gained their loyalty through conquest—the notable thorn in his flesh was Rana Pratap, the Sisodia king who refused an alliance and never surrendered. Akbar died in 1605, leaving an empire which covered most of India north of the River Godavari.

Jahangir: Akbar's son and successor who matured into a cultured hedonist. The Mughal court was by now luxurious and lavish and the emperor could lead a pampered life. Jahangir's senior wife, Nur Jahan ('Light of the World'), became virtual ruler of the empire and his sons attempted coups against the throne. Sir Thomas Roe, ambassador to King James I of England, spent four years in Jahangir's court and managed to secure trading rights. His achievements eased England's way into India. Jahangir died in 1627; there followed a year of intrigue and uncertainty as the potential successors promoted their claims for the emperorship.

The man who built the Taj Mahal

Shah Jahan: Son of Jahangir and a Rajput princess, Shah Jahan inherited the throne in 1628. He expanded the empire in the east and south of India, but he is best remembered as a great builder, and especially for the construction of the Taj Mahal, a mausoleum for his wife Mumtaz Mahal ('Jewel of the Palace') who died in 1631. Shah Jahan's illness in his last years encouraged palace intrigue amongst his sons and, indeed, Aurangzeb kept his father imprisoned until his death in 1666.

Aurangzeb: A powerful prince who ascended the throne before the death of his father Emperor Shah Jahan. Under Aurangzeb the Mughal empire reached its greatest extent and covered all of India except the very southern tip. Aurangzeb was an Islamic zealot—he imposed the jiziya tax on non-Moslems and did much to undermine Hindu culture by destroying temples and treating believers with complete disdain. He attacked Rajputana and, after the death of Jaswant Singh, he waged a 30-year war against the Rathores of Jodhpur with the hope of annexing Marwar; he met greater success in Mewar after signing a treaty with the once unreconcilable Sisodias. Aurangzeb died in 1707, aged 90.

The Later Mughals: After Aurangzeb there was the typical power struggle with Bahadur Shah winning the title of emperor. But by now the Mughal dynasty was in decline, its leaders were of lesser substance than their illustrious predecessors and proved too weak against their many opponents. The line of emperors finally petered out with the demise of Bahadur Shah II in 1862, but by then the Mughals had long lost their empire and any real authority.

Glossary

Agni: Fire.

Agnivansh: The Fire Born clan of Rajputs originating from the fire pit at Mount Abu; it includes the Chauhan and Harachauhan clans.

Angam: A courtyard.

Apsaras: The heavenly nymphets in Hindu mythology.
Arti: A prayer session.
Aryan: The peoples, probably originating from the steppes of Russia, who invaded the Indian subcontinent in the second millenium BC.
Ashram: A spiritual retreat and a place of learning, especially associated with meditation and yogism.
Avatar: An incarnation of a god.
Baba: A religious master, though it is also a term of respect usually addressed to an older man.
Bagh: A garden.
Baoli: A well; often an elaborate construction with steps leading down to the water.
Bhagavad Gita: An important religious (Hindu) text, and a section of the Mahabharata, in which Krishna expounds his philosophies. It includes fundamental lessons in yoga and bhakti.
Bhakti: Pure love and adoration.
Bhandar: A treasury.
Bhatti: The ruling Rajput clan from Jaisalmer.
Bhavan: A large house or building.
Bhopa: Itinerant balladist.
Bodhisattva: A follower of Buddha; a buddhist who attains a position worthy of enlightenment.
Brahma: One of the great Hindu trinity; Brahma is the Creator of the Universe.
Brahmin: The highest of the four Hindu caste groups; traditionally Brahmins are priests.
Buddha: Prince Gautama Siddhartha lived from approximately 612 BC to 488 BC. His doctrines are embodied in Buddhism.
Buddhism: The ultimate aim of Buddhism is to attain nirvana and the core of its ethics is Buddha's Noble Eightfold Path: 1) Right comprehension (freedom from prejudices, illusions and superstitions); 2) right resolution (pressing forward to a higher goal); 3) right speech (kindly, faithful, true); 4) right conduct (peace-loving, honest, pure); 5) right living (harmless livelihood, hurting no living thing); 6) right effort (perseverance in well-doing); 7) right meditation (intellectual activity, always directed to

Rule and Doctrine); 8) right rapture (intense reflection, the mind being wholly withdrawn from things of time and sense).

Bund: A causeway or embankment.

Burj: A fortified tower.

Cantonment: An old military or office enclave created during the days of the British Raj.

Caravanserai: A hostel providing accommodation for travelling caravans.

Caste system: The Hindus' social hierarchy. A person is born into a caste (from the Portuguese *casta* meaning pure) which reflects a relative degree of purity; in other words, his social standing in the community. There are four castes (these are divided into numerous sub-castes): top of the list are the Brahmins: the priests and religious teachers; next the Kshatriyas: royalty, nobles and warriors (these include the Rajputs); third are the Vaisyas: merchants and traders; and finally the Sudras: farmers. Outside the caste system, too 'impure' to be part of it, are the Untouchables, now euphemistically called Harijans.

Chandra: Moon, hence Chandrapol: Moon Gate.

Chattri: A tomb, mausoleum. Literally an umbrella.

Chauhans: The Rajput clan which once ruled Delhi and Ajmer.

Choli: The blouse worn by women under their sari.

Chowk: A market place.

Dargah: A shrine or tomb of a Moslem saint.

Darshan: Usually refers to an audience with a guru.

Deori: A gate.

Devi: The Great Mother, consort of Shiva; devi also means goddess.

Dharamsala: A lodge for itinerant pilgrims.

Dharma: Buddhist teachings. Dharma also refers to the universal law which controls a person's life, e.g. caste, social codes.

Dhoti: The cloth commonly worn by men which is wrapped around the waist and then fastened only by folds and tucks.

Diwan: A court; also a chief minister in a princely state.

Diwan-I-Am: Hall of Public Audience.
Diwan-I-Khas: Hall of Private Audience.
Durbar: Assembly of princes at a royal court.
Durrie: A mat, often used as bedding by travellers.
Fakir: A religious—more correctly a Moslem—mendicant.
Gaadi: A throne.
Ganesh: The Hindu god with a head of an elephant. Son of Shiva and Parvati, the popular Ganesh is the patron of good fortune.
Ganga: The River Ganges, the most sacred of rivers for Hindus.
Garh: A fort, hence Chittorgarh.
Garuda: Mythical creature with aspects of a bird—a sort of eagle—but the body of a man. Garuda is the vehicle of the god Vishnu.
Gaumukh: The mouth of the sacred cow.
Gautama: The personal name of Buddha.
Ghat: The flight of steps on the bank of a river leading down to the water.
Gopis: The cow girls often seen in the paintings of Krishna.
Guptas: The dynasty of kings who ruled in India from AD 320 to 540.
Guru: A spiritual teacher.
Hanuman: The monkey god.
Harachauhans: The Rajput clan which settled in the Haravati region of southeast Rajasthan; they are sometimes known as the Haras.
Harijan: A title given to the Untouchables, the non-caste people at the bottom of the Hindu social hierarchy, literally meaning 'Children of God'. The term was introduced by Mahatma Gandhi in his attempt to erode the stigma attached to these people, who were destined to the most menial of lives through the fate of their birth.
Haveli: A grand house, the traditional style mansion.
Hawa: Wind, hence Hawa Mahal, Palace of Wind.
Hindi: The language most predominantly spoken in India and the nation's lingua franca.
Hindu: Literally a native of Hindustan, the country

of the upper valley of the Ganges, though more usually Hindu refers to a follower of Hinduism.

Hinduism: The predominant religion in India and adhered to by 80% of the population. Hinduism originated some 3000 years ago and evolved into a complex social organisation as well as a religion. Hindus believe that their spirit is reincarnated through a succession of lives, until they finally reach their moksha or spiritual salvation from worldly existences. The Holy Trinity comprising Brahma the Creator, Vishnu the Preserver and Shiva the Destroyer and hence reproducer for a future incarnation, head a huge pantheon of gods. The lesser deities are in fact closely associated with the Trinity, being consorts, companions or incarnations of the Big Three. Shrines and temples to the gods are found everywhere and they are piously venerated by devotees. Hinduism lays down exact social codes and, as they are strictly followed by Hindus, they provide cohesion in the community.

Howdah: The seat on top of an elephant to carry passengers.

Imam: The prayer leader in a mosque.

Indra: The storm god; Indra is one of the ancient Vedic deities.

Islam: The principal belief of Islam is the existence of one God, the same God worshipped by Christians and Jews, whom Moslems call Allah. Islam means submission. Moslem means one who submits to monotheism as interpreted by the religion's founder, Mohammed (AD 570–632).

Jai: Victory, hence Jai Stambha, Tower of Victory.

Jain: A follower of Jainism.

Jainism: A Hindu religion based on the teachings of Mahavira (599–527 BC), the 24th and last Tirthankar or prophet. Jainism has a similar philosophy to Buddhism and prescribes non-violence as its fundamental edict. Wishing no harm to fellow animals, Jains are strict vegetarians; indeed, the stauncher adherents mask their mouths to avoid accidentally swallowing the smaller insects. The Jain temples at Ranakpur and Dilwara (Mount Abu) are marvellously crafted monuments.

Jantar Mantar: The masonry observatory built by Sawai Jai Singh in Jaipur; there is another Jantar Mantar in Delhi.

Ji (-ji): A suffix denoting respect, for example: Gandhiji, Babaji, Peterji, etc.

Jiziya: The tax prescribed by some of the Mughal emperors on non-Moslems.

Johar: The horrific mass immolation practised by Rajput women who preferred to die in this honourable fashion rather than be taken as captives.

Johari: Jeweller, hence Johari Bazaar, Jewellers' Bazaar.

Kadi: Homespun cloth.

Kali: An incarnation of Devi or Parvati in the fearful form of the goddess of death and destruction. Kali also means black.

Karma: A person's fate, which is prescribed to them by the supernatural powers according to the way they behaved in their past life.

Khana: An armoury.

Khush: Happiness, hence Khush Mahal, Palace of Happiness.

Krishna: The eighth incarnation of Vishnu. He is usually depicted with blue skin and often he is playing a flute. Krishna is the principal character in the Bhagavad Gita and he has a large following, which includes sects like the Hare Krishna.

Kshatriya: The second of the Hindu castes; kshatriyas are traditionally kings, nobles and warriors.

Kuchwaha: The Rajput clan who ruled the Dhundar region of Rajasthan with capitals at Amber and then Jaipur.

Lal: Red, hence Lalgarh, Red Fort.

Laxmi: Vishnu's consort and the goddess of wealth.

Lingam: The phallus, a symbol of Shiva which represents fertility and strength.

Lok Kala: Folk art.

Longhi: A length of material which men wrap around their waist as an equivalent of a loin cloth.

Maha: Great. It is usually a prefix, hence Maharaja,

Great Raja.

Mahabharata: One of the two ancient epic Vedic poems which was first written between 400 BC and AD 200, though orally it dates to an earlier age.

Mahal: A palace, or a queen.

Mahatma: A great soul, e.g. Mahatma Gandhi.

Maharaja: A great ruler or king. A maharani is a queen.

Maharana: The title given to the maharaja of the Sisodia clan from Mewar.

Maidan: A public gardens or open space.

Manak: Ruby, hence Manak Mahal, Ruby Palace.

Mandir: A temple; also a hall or gallery.

Mantra: A holy chant.

Marg: A road or avenue; sometimes it means a field.

Marwaris: Literally people from the Thar Desert region of Marwar. More colloquially it refers to the business or entrepreneurial class originating from the Shekavati district.

Masjid: A principal mosque.

Mata: Mother.

Maurayans: The ancient and powerful dynasty of Indian kings who ruled from 322 BC to 183 BC.

Memsahibs: A term of respect or courtesy addressed to ladies, rather like the French use of madame.

Meenakari: Enamel work.

Mela: A festival.

Mendhi: The dye used by women to decorate their hands and feet.

Mogri: A hill.

Moksha: The attainment of nirvana when a person/spirit breaks off the shackles of secular existence.

Monsoons: The seasonal rains which sweep across the country between June and October.

Moslem: See Islam.

Moti: Pearl, hence Moti Mahal, Pearl Palace.

Mughals: The dynasty of Moslem emperors which ruled much of the sub-continent from the time when Barbur, its founder, invaded India and defeated local resistence at the Battle of Panipat (1526) until the death of Aurangzeb in 1707.

Mullah: A Moslem teacher or interpreter of religious law.
Naga: The snake in Hindu mythology.
Namaste: The traditional greeting: press the palms of your hands together with the fingers pointing upwards.
Nandi: The bull, the vehicle for Shiva.
Nirvana: The ultimate state for Buddhists (the term is also used by Hindus) when they have broken free from secular existence, no longer to suffer the cycle of rebirths.
Niwas: A house, sometimes implying accommodation: also a palace.
Pahar: A mountain.
Palaquin: A covered litter in which a person sits; it is suspended from poles and these are borne on the shoulders of men.
Pandit: A scholar or teacher.
Phool: Flower, hence Phool Mahal, Flower Palace.
Pichwai: A painting on cloth and a typical handicraft from Udaipur.
Pol: A gate.
Prasad: An offering of food, usually to a god at a temple or to a holy man.
Puja: Offerings or prayers to the gods.
Pukkah: Correct in terms of etiquette and decorum; the expression was commonly used in the days of the British Raj.
Puranas: Old Sanskrit texts written in the form of myths and legends.
Purdah: A traditional Moslem practice, later adopted by high caste Hindus, when women confine themselves to their own quarters, out of the view of men.
Purnima: Full moon night.
Raga: Any of a number of traditional melody patterns used as source material for improvisation.
Raj: Rule; it most frequently refers to the British rule in India.
Raja: A king. Rani is a queen.
Rajput: Literally the 'Sons of Princes'; the Rajputs are kshatriyas and their clans ruled Rajputana.

Several main ragas were endowed with a family of 'wives' (raginis)—this lady, representing a ragini, is preparing to meet her lover

Rajputana: Literally the 'Land of Princes', a region which comprised a collection of independent princely states in northwest India. After Independence the states united under the Indian flag and Rajputana was renamed Rajasthan.
Rama: Hero of the Ramayana.
Ramayana: A Sanskrit epic—written down between 200 BC and AD 200, though dating from an earlier period—which relates how king Rama, helped by Hanuman the monkey, rescued his wife Sita from the demon Ravana who lived in Lanka (Sri Lanka).
Rana: The title given to the raja of the Sisodia clan from Mewar.
Rani: A queen.
Rao: The title given to the raja of the Rathore clans from Jodhpur and Bikaner and also the raja of the Bhatti clan from Jaisalmer.
Rathores: The ruling Rajput clan of Jodhpur and also of Bikaner.
Rickshaw: A local means of transport around towns: essentially a tricycle with passengers sitting on the back. The auto-rickshaw is the motorised version.
Rishi: A sage or philosopher, especially one who has supernatural powers.
Sadhu: A roving holy man in search of religious salvation; a Hindu ascetic.
Safed: White.
Sagar: A lake.
Sahib: Master, the rough equivalent of the English 'sir' as an address of respect.
Sajjan: Lotus.
Sanskrit: Ancient Indian language with origins in the Indo-European group. Many of the old Indian epics and texts were written in Sanskrit.
Sari: A 6-metre length of material worn by women.
Sati: The ritual followed by the newly widowed woman: she immolates herself by mounting her husband's funeral pyre. The practice was banned by the British in 1829, but even today there are occasional reports of women committing sati.
Sati hands: Before committing sati, women—especially the wives of royalty—would leave an

imprint of their hand on a wall.

Shakti: Spiritual energy.

Shaivite: A follower of Shiva.

Sheesh: Mirror, hence Sheesh Mahal, Palace of Mirrors.

Shikar: A peak or pinnacle.

Shiva: One of the gods in the great Hindu Trinity. Shiva is the Destroyer, but he also represents creative energy. There are more temples to Shiva than to any other Hindu god.

Sisodia: The ruling Rajput clan of Mewar.

Sitar: An elaborate stringed musical instrument.

Stambha: Tower.

Sukh: Pleasure, hence Sukh Mahal, Pleasure Palace.

Surya/Suraj: Sun, hence Surajpol, Sun Gate.

Suryavansh: The Solar clans of Rajputs which include the Sisodias, Rathores and Kuchwahas.

Tabla: A small drum.

Tank: A water reservoir or artificial lake.

Tara: Star, hence Taragarh, Star Fort.

Tikka: The dot of powder or paste on the forehead of married Hindu woman.

Tirthankars: The 24 Jain prophets.

Tonga: A bullock- or horse-drawn cart serving as a means of transport.

Topi: A sun hat, also the pith helmet worn by the British.

Upanishad: Sanskrit texts in which ancient religious doctrines are outlined; they are last part of the Vedas.

Urs: Moslem festival.

Vaishnavite: A follower of Vishnu.

Vedas: The most ancient of Hindu scriptures, probably composed in the second millenium BC.

Vilas: A palace, house or residence.

Vimana: The main part of a Hindu temple.

Vishnu: One of the gods of the great Hindu Trinity. Vishnu is the Preserver.

Wallah: Meaning man, hence Dhobi-wallah, washerman; rickshaw-wallah, rickshaw man; etc.

Yantra: An astronomical instrument, such as those in the Jantar Mantar.

Yoga: Literally means effort or union, and through meditation and precisely choreographed exercises the individual reaches a spiritual peace.
Yogi: One who practices yoga.
Zenana: The women's quarters in a house, which are usually out of bounds to men; also a harem.

PRACTICAL BACKGROUND

Tourist Information

Information abroad

The Government of India Tourism Development Corporation (ITDC) has offices all around India, including Rajasthan, and they can give you information on the whole country and its parts. The Indian government also has tourist offices abroad and these include:

Australia:
Carlton Centre
55 Elizabeth Street
Sydney, NSW 2000
Tel: 02 232 1600
and
8 Parliament Court
1076 Hay Street
West Perth, WA 6005
Tel: 06 321 6932

Britain:
7 Cork Street
London W1X QAB
Tel: 01-437 3677/8

Canada:
Suite 1016
Royal Trust Tower
(PO Box 342)
Toronto Dominion Centre
Toronto, Ontario MSK IK7
Tel: 416 362 3188

France:
8 Boulevard de la Madelaine
75009 Paris
Tel: 265 8386

USA:
30 Rockafeller Plaza
15 North Mezzanine
New York, NY 10020
Tel: 212 586 4901
and
201 North Michigan Avenue
Chicago, Illinois 60601
Tel: 312 236 6899
and
3550 Wilshire Boulevard
(Suite 204)
Los Angeles, California 90010
Tel: 213 380 8855

West Germany:
Kaiserstrasse 77–111
6 Frankfurt Main
Tel: 232 380

Information in India

The Rajasthan Tourism Development Corporation (RTDC) deals specifically with Rajasthan and has offices at the regional capitals and places of tourist interest around the state. The local tourist officer can give you details on accommodation, restaurants, transport, markets, sights, tours, etc, in his catchment area. He can also give you brochures on the other parts of Rajasthan. Generally these officers are a useful source of information for both the mundane and the unusual.

RTDC Offices in Rajasthan and elsewhere in India:

Agra
10 New Shopping Arcade
Near Taj Mahal
Tel: 64582

Ahmedabad
4 Karmavati Society
Ashram Road
Tel: 405289

Ajmer
Khadim Tourist Bungalow
Savitri Girls' College Road
Tel: 21626

Alwar
Information Centre
Near Purjan Vihar Garden
Tel: 3863

Amber
Near Elephant Stand
Tel: 40764

Bharatpur
Circuit House
Agra Road
Tel: 2340

Bikaner
Junagarh Fort
Poonam Singh Circle
Tel: 5445

Bombay
230 Dr DN Road
Tel: 2044162

Bundi
Near Collectorate
Tel: 301

Calcutta
Third Floor
135 Canning Street
Tel: 279051

Chittor
Janta Avas Grih
Tel: 9

Jaipur
Head Office (administration)
100 Jawaharlal Nehru Marg
Jaipur 302 004
Tel: 73873/7485
and
Railway Station
Tel: 69714
and
Central Bus Station
Sindhi Camp

Jodhpur
Ghoomar Tourist Bungalow
Tel: 251183

Jaisalmer
Moomal Tourist Bungalow
Tel: 106

Kotah
Chambal Tourist Bungalow
Tel: 26527

Madras
28 Commander-in-Chief Road
Tel: PP 812955

Mount Abu
Opposite Bus Stand
Tel: 51

New Delhi
Chandralok Building
36 Janpath
Tel: 322332/321820

Sawai Madhopur
Project Tiger
Castle Jhoomar Baori
Tel: PP 23

Udaipur
Kajri Tourist Bungalow
Shastri Circle
Tel: 23605
and
Dabok Airport
Tel: PP 23011
and
Railway Station

How to Get There

The closest international airport to Rajasthan is at New Delhi, India's capital, from where you can take an internal flight or travel by train or bus into Rajasthan (see *Travel Within Rajasthan*, below).

Several airlines besides Air India and British Airways fly between London and New Delhi and the air fare can vary tremendously. Even if you are not originating your journey in Britain, it may pay to purchase your ticket in London which is an international clearing house for discounted fares. Recommended in this respect is Trailfinders (42–48 Earls Court Road, London W8 6EJ; Tel: 01-938 3366), a reliable discount ticket agency. Savings of 33 percent are easily possible on return fares, London-New Delhi-London, or a visit to Rajasthan can be incorporated into a wider Asian travel programme.

Getting there for less

Tour operators in Britain and elsewhere offer package holidays to Rajasthan. For up to date information consult your travel agent or one of the India Government Tourist Offices abroad.

Visa Requirements

Foreigners—Britons and Commonwealth citizens included—need visas for entry into India.

In England visas are obtainable from:

The Indian High Commission
India House
Aldwych
London WC2B 4NA
Tel: 01-836 8484

There is also a visa department in Birmingham. Contact 021-643 0366 for details.

On applying for a visa you must fill in an application form, submit three passport size photographs and a valid passport.

The visa costs £20 for a single entry (£40 for a double entry) and is valid for six months from the date of issue; it will allow you up to a three-month stay from the day you set foot in India. Payment for visas must be made in cash (or postal order); cheques and credit cards are not accepted.

Delivery times at the High Commission are 09.30 to 13.00 and you can collect your visa the following day between 16.30 and 17.30. You can apply by post, however they suggest you allow four weeks for delivery.

The Indian embassies in Australia and the USA are at the following addresses:

92 Mugga Way
Red Hill
ACT 2603, Australia
Tel: 062 95 0045

2107 Massachusetts Avenue NW
Washington DC 2008, USA
Tel: 265 5050

Climate

There are three distinct seasons in India: the hot, the monsoon and the cool.

The hot season in Rajasthan starts in March, reaching almost unbearable temperatures towards the end of May, the beginning of June. The dry, blasting heat and the hazy skies are most severe in the desert; this is the time when those who can will retreat up to Mount Abu, Rajasthan's hill station, where the climate is cooler and far more pleasant.

If on time, the monsoons arrive in the second week of June. Their heavy rains bring life back to the parched soils—and a huge sense of relief to everyone: failure of the monsoons will lead to drought. The rain falls daily in short torrential bursts and once over the skies clear and the sun shines warmly; it is not an unpleasant time to visit Rajasthan.

The best season

The rains ease off in September and herald the best season. From October Rajasthan is dry, lush, pleasantly cool (temperatures are similar to a good north European summer), clear skied and sunny. The nights get chilly, especially in the desert. The

	Altitude (metres)	Temperatures Summer Mean Max.	Mean Min.	Winter Mean Max.	Mean Min.	Rainfall (centimetres)	Best Season
Jaipur	431	41°C	26°C	22°C	8°C	64	October–March
Bharatpur	205	45°C	37°C	32°C	22°C	69	October–March
Alwar	268	37°C	24°C	31°C	11°C	64	October–March
Ajmer	486	44°C	38°C	23°C	16°C	57	October–March
Bundi	302	42°C	36°C	32°C	12°C	67	October–March
Kotah	250	42°C	36°C	32°C	12°C	70	October–March
Udaipur	577	33°C	23°C	28°C	12°C	61	October–March
Chittor	408	34°C	23°C	28°C	12°C		October–March
Mount Abu	1219	33°C	17°C	25°C	7°C	170	Mid-March—July Mid-September–Mid-November
Jodhpur	230	42°C	37°C	26°C	16°C	31	October–February
Bikaner	237	42°C	28°C	23°C	10°C	44	October–February
Jaisalmer	225	46°C	35°C	14°C	1°C	28	October–February

coolest months are December and January; in February the temperatures pick up and by the end of March the heat has become uncomfortable.

What to Wear

A great advantage of travelling in hot countries is that there is no need for the heavy and sometimes specialised clothing that is required for cold climates. Thus weight and initial expenditure should be minimal.

Travelling light

A few changes of light cotton clothing is all that is required, though surplus T-shirts and jeans can be exchanged or given as presents along the way. If necessary additional clothes, including Western-style garments, can easily be bought in Rajasthan; indeed, you may wish to have some clothes made by a local tailor. Some travellers forfeit their usual attire for the 'native' garb.

Winter nights can get a bit nippy, especially in the desert, so it is advisable to take a light pullover (easily purchased in India if necessary).

Track/gym shoes, espaddrilles and flip flops (easily washed) are suggested footwear. Excellent and inexpensive leather sandals are available everywhere and shoes can be made to order.

Scantily-clad Westerners, particularly women, can cause offence and could be the butt of a few jokes. It is polite as well as advisable to dress conservatively in public places: women should be prepared to wear below-the-knee dresses.

Before entering a temple or mosque you may be requested to take off your shoes and also leave any leather articles (bags, watches and cameras with leather straps, etc) at the entrance.

Health

There are no vaccination requirements for visitors to India—save for yellow fever and smallpox vaccinations if you are coming from an infected area.

Vaccinations, etc

However, vaccinations, inoculations or tablets are officially recommended to help prevent travellers contracting cholera, malaria, typhoid, polio and yellow fever. In some cases courses of vaccination, etc, are ideally started at least two months before departure. In other cases all you will need is a booster to regain protection if you have been vaccinated in recent years. So it is best to see your doctor at an early stage.

Cholera is contracted through contaminated food and water. Prevention consists of either one injection or two taken about two weeks apart. It is effective for six months, though there is no certainty of complete protection.

Malaria is transmitted by a bite from an infected mosquito. It is recommended that anti-malaria tablets are taken (either daily or weekly, depending on the type of prophylaxis). Start the dosage just before entering an infected area and continue the course of tablets for 28 days after leaving it. Your doctor will advise you on the most suitable brand of malaria tablets.

Polio is usually contracted from an already infected person, but also from contaminated food and water. Prevention is in the form of three doses of drops, normally administered on sugar lumps, taken four to six weeks apart. It is effective for ten years.

Typhoid is caught from contaminated food, water and milk. Prevention is achieved by two injections taken four to six weeks apart (though the period can be reduced to ten days). It is effective for three years.

Tetanus is contracted from contaminated soil, manure, dirty (e.g. rusty) objects and finds entry into the body through a wound. Two injections six weeks apart allows one year's protection; a booster six to 12 months after the initial course gives a ten-year immunity.

Yellow fever is caught from the bite of a contaminated mosquito. One injection should be administered at least ten days before arriving in a risk area. It is effective for ten years. The vaccination is given at certain clinics only; the ones in central London are mentioned below. Some doctors advise a period of several weeks between taking gamma globulin see infectious hepatitis) and vaccinations for yellow fever.

The World Health Organisation has declared that *smallpox* has been eradicated worldwide.

Infectious hepatitis is caught from contaminated water, food or even people (for example the disease can be contracted from an infected colleague if you share a common spoon, glass, cigarette, etc). When in a place which seems unhygienic make sure that raw vegetables and unpeeled fruits have been washed in purified water and do not drink untreated water. Gamma globulin is the vaccination against hepatitis, though its effectiveness is not total. Seek advice from your doctor.

Rabies is the result of a bite or scratch from an infected animal (avoid familiarity with animals, however inocuous they may seem). There are injections which provide some protection against the disease. Consult your doctor for further details.

Clinics

Your local doctor should be able to vaccinate you against cholera, polio, typhoid and tetanus and he can give you a prescription for the relevant malaria tablets. Alternatively the following clinics in London will give you all the jabs—including the yellow fever vaccination—and tablets you require; the doctors at these centres are experts on health care in hot climates. The National Health surgeries will charge less for their services than the privately run clinics.

British Airways Immunisation Centres
Heathrow Airport
Tel: 01-750 5453
74 Regents Street
London W1
Tel: 01-439 9584

Medical Department
Unilever House
Blackfriars
London EC4
Tel: 01-822 6017

Hospital for Tropical Diseases
4 St Pancras Way
London NW1
Tel: 01-387 4411

Vaccination Service
53 Great Cumberland Place
London W1
Tel: 01-262 6456

Precautions *Food*: Avoid raw vegetables and unpeeled fruits unless you know that they have been washed properly. Be careful of salads if the restaurant has poor hygienic standards. Uncooked, cold or reheated food is susceptible to contamination, so try and eat freshly cooked food.

Water: Avoid tap water. If you have doubts anywhere about the cleanliness of the drinking water then boil it—or sterilise it by adding iodine solution or (less effective) water purifying tablets. Diseases can be caught from glasses or cutlery washed in unclean water. Also be wary of ice cream and ice used to cool your drink. To be on the safe side it is often worth paying a little for a cup of tea or a bottled drink.

Cuts: Wash and treat all cuts and grazes immediately. An antiseptic solution like TCP should be carried in addition to antisceptic cream (the latter is greasy and attracts dirt, but is useful at times). Some doctors recommend applying stronger antibiotic powder to wounds. Cover cuts to avoid exposure to dirt.

Sun: Protection against the sun like a hat, a good pair of sunglasses (preferably polarised) and a lotion which acts as a barrier against ultraviolet light is recommended. If there is a chance that you will suffer badly under the sun (e.g. sunburn) then ask your doctor for the necessary medicaments before your departure. Be sensible about exposing your body to the sun and do so in gradual stages if you are not used to it. During the winter months the heat is by no means unbearable.

Bites: Insect repellant cream helps ward off mosquitoes. Mosquito nets are useful, and most hotels will be able to provide you with one when required.

Diarrhoea: The most effective way to cure diarrhoea is to eat as little as possible and drink lots of fluid. A recommended concoction is a glass of fruit juice with a pinch of salt and a teaspoonful of sugar. Drink tea if you have no alternative and if you have doubts about the purity of the water. Doctors will advise you on the medicines which prevent and cure diarrhoea. Also ask your doctor how to distinguish diarrhoea from dysentery and how to treat the different types of the latter disease. Fresh onions/garlic and lemons can be recommended as a specific against stomach upsets.

If you do get seriously ill go to a hospital—or to a doctor who has been recommended to you by the local pharmacist or top hotel or other reliable source; avoid quacks. Take a basic first aid kit, and you may feel happier with your own selection of brand name medicaments rather than trusting the locally available unknown alternatives.

Insurance

Medical insurance (and insurance against the loss of personal belongings) is recommended. Thomas Cook (policies can be drawn out at any of their travel agencies) and Endsleigh Insurance Services Limited, Cranfield House, 97–107 Southampton Row, London WC1; Tel: 01-580 4311 (head London branch), are two companies experienced in travel insurance.

There are various publications which will give you useful information and hints on how to protect your health when abroad; here are just a few: *The Travellers' Health Guide* by A C Turner; *Preservation of Personal Health in Warm Climates*, issued by the Ross Institute, Keppel Street, London (Tel: 01-636 8636); *Protect Your Health Abroad*, issued by the Department of Health and Social Security.

Money

The rupee (Rs), the Indian unit of currency, is divided into 100 paise (p). There are coins of 1, 2, 3, 5, 10, 20, 25 and 50 paise. And notes of 1, 2, 5, 10, 20, 50, 100 and 500 rupees. The exchange rate is approximately: £1 = 23 Rs.

You are not allowed to bring rupees into India, nor can you take them out of the country. You may bring as much foreign currency/travellers' cheques into India as you wish and—in theory at least—the

Exchanging money

amount should be declared on arrival if over $1000. It is probably wiser to take sterling or US dollars as these are the foreign currencies Indians are most familiar with; similarly, a better known brand name of travellers' cheque—such as American Express or Thomas Cook—should be recognised wherever you go, while the more obscure ones may not.

Changing cash or travellers' cheques in a bank, especially in the smaller towns, tends to be a laborious process as for each transaction you are required to fill in various forms, which then have to be signed by different members of staff, before you are finally given your rupees. So it is worth keeping your visits to the bank down to the minimum.

Alternatively, go to one of the better hotels where they exchange money—it is usually quicker, though the rate probably won't be as favourable. Keep your currency exchange forms as they are proof that you have changed your money legally and you may be asked to present them if you want to buy, for example, a plane ticket in rupees; you will also need them if you reconvert surplus rupees back into foreign currency.

There is a black market, though it is not so glaringly obvious as in some countries. A shopkeeper may give you a discount if you pay for a purchase in hard currency.

Change is hard to come by in India, so get a supply of coins and low denomination banknotes from the bank—they are useful for bus fares, buying a cup of tea, giving as a tip, etc. Avoid being given torn or badly creased notes—few shopkeepers will accept them; however the banks will change them for newer notes if you do get caught out.

Credit cards

Credit cards are accepted at the fancier hotels and shops and also for the purchase of plane tickets: American Express and Diners Club are the most favoured, though you can also use Visa and Mastercharge/Access at a reasonable number of places.

Tipping is obviously up to the individual, but

The Rambagh Palace Hotel at Jaipur

as a rough rule of thumb: it is not necessary to tip taxi drivers or waiters—nor the hotel staff, unless, of course, you feel they have given you particular attention (in the more expensive hotels a service charge may well be included in your bill). At stations/airports you pay the porter a set rate per bag he carries. The going tarrif is usually posted on a board or otherwise ask a local.

Time

Indian Standard Time is 5½ hours ahead of Greenwich Mean Time (i.e. noon GMT = 17.30 IST), 4½ hours behind Australian Eastern Standard Time and 10½ hours ahead of American Eastern Standard Time.

Electricity

Voltage in India is usually 220. It is worth having a flashlight for when the electricity fails.

Accommodation

As with everything in India, accommodation reaches the utter extremes of the spectrum. At one end you have exceedingly lavish palace hotels—unique to India and amongst the most indulgent hotels anywhere—where bearers and servants pamper guests as if they were maharajas and maharanis. At the other end there are squalid bug infested hotels which are probably best avoided. Fortunately cheapness does not mean squalor and the low budget traveller can find ample clean and inexpensive places to stay. Between the two extremes there is a variety of mid-range accommodation to chose from.

You have a reasonable selection of hotels of all standards in the major cities, but once you get off the beaten track your choice can be very limited.

Palace hotels. Since Independence the maharajas have lost their power, privileges, privy purses and much of the time honoured status they enjoyed amongst their subjects. Nevertheless they remain respected figureheads of their clans and, for the tourists at least, they serve as romantic anachronisms and essential components of the exotic Orient.

Many erstwhile royalty still own and reside in their family palaces, but in order to pay for the maintenance they have had to convert their magnificent and historic homes into hotels.

The palace hotels are of varying standards. Some are run by international hotel chains and have been tastefully refurbished, combining traditional decor with all the mod cons to produce luxurious, efficient, first rate hotels which are amongst the finest and most stylish in India. Others are more modest—and less expensive—but are full of dusty nostalgia and have a marvellous easy going atmosphere.

The best palace hotels

Four luxurious palace hotels stand out above the rest: the Rambagh Palace (Jaipur), the Umaid Bhawan Palace (Jodhpur), the Lake Palace and the Shiv Niwas (both Udaipur). See the relevant chapters.

Other types of accommodation. There are some modern hotels in the bigger cities—the better ones are run by the top hotel chains—but however good they may be they will seem a dull substitute for a palace hotel.

At places of tourist interest you will find a state-run **Tourist Bungalow.** After you have travelled Rajasthan for a while you will look upon the 'Bungalow' as a welcoming and dependable friend; often in the remoter corners no other accommodation exists. They may be drab inside—sometimes shabby and dirty—but you can rely on them being of an acceptable standard, with certain facilities like air-conditioned rooms and private bathrooms. They offer you a modest selection of wholesome Indian food (their Western dishes may not be so successful) and good chilled drinking water; and if all their rooms are occupied you can always stay in the dormitory.

Most of the Bungalows are modern constructions (exceptions include the attractively converted hunting lodge at Sawai Madhopur) and some have recently been redecorated, while others are in desperate need of a lick of paint. Their uniformity of style can get monotonous. The prices are reasonable and standard. Even cheaper and simpler are the government-run Rest Houses. They are smaller and more basic versions of the Bungalow and tend to be located in off-beat places.

Other government-run accommodation includes the **Circuit Houses,** which provide senior Indian officials with a place to stay when they are travelling Rajasthan on duty. Some are rather grand, built by the British as regional headquarters, and they still echo something of the Raj—despite the addition of tacky modern furnishings and decor. The manager can only open his doors to non-officials after the officials have been accommodated.

DAK Bungalows operate on the same basis as the Circuit Houses, but they are for the less senior officials travelling on duty. Standards are much more basic and in some obscure places the DAK is the only accommodation you will find. Once again the availability of rooms depends on the day's quota of travelling officials. The rates are very reasonable at both the Circuit Houses and DAK Bungalows.

The **Railway Retiring Rooms** offer the basic facilities of a hotel in the station itself. The inexpensive rooms or dormitories are clean and simple—many a Retiring Room still has a definate flavour of the Raj. They serve as ideal accommodation for anyone with an early morning train to catch—indeed you need a valid train ticket to stay here. The cacophony down on the platform and the sound of steam trains passing through the night is a curse to most slumberers, but it is music to the ears of the serious train buff and the experience is something he should not miss. Just make sure there are night services stopping at your station!

For train buffs

The **Railway Waiting Room**—preferably the First Class Room—is a reasonable enough place to try and get a few hours sleep before catching one of those middle of the night trains.

Dharamsalas are hostels built by the rich to provide accommodation for pilgrims and impoverished (Indian) travellers. Rooms and dormitories are usually extremely basic and often you are expected to provide your own bedding. You pay only a few rupees or sometimes you can stay for free, but it should be remembered that many dharamsalas are charitable institutions and should not be abused by freeloading Westerners.

The cheap hotels and lodges so often frequented by (Western) travellers are fairly easy to find in the main cities and new ones are popping up all the time. They vary considerably in standard and cleanliness, but, as a yardstick, you can get a room with fan and shower and loo for between 25 Rs and 100 Rs a night—and that may be for one, two or three people. Travellers congregate at the 'in' place of the time and you will hear about the best of the cheap hotels through word of mouth recommendation; alternatively ask at the Tourist Office.

The price of a room. The hotels mentioned in this book have been placed into price brackets according to the tariff of a double room. These are very rough catagorisations and it is worth noting that in, for example, a Tourist Bungalow you may pay 150 Rs for a room with air conditioning, but you can also find a bed in their dormitory for under 20 Rs.

Upper range	250 Rs and over
Mid-range	100–250 Rs
Lower range	100 Rs and below

The top 'international standard' hotels—such as the smarter palace hotels mentioned above—charge way in excess of 250 Rs. Expect to pay from 750 Rs for a double up to 3000 Rs for a suite. The Shiv Niwas at Udaipur, the most exquisite hotel of all, is even more expensive.

What you get for your money

In some hotels there are tariffs for American Plan (AP), Modified American Plan (MAP) and European Plan (EP)—in other words: full board, half board and bed and breakfast respectively. Sometimes it is obligatory to take one of these 'plans', so it is worth knowing what you are paying for.

Rooms in the upper range hotels have air conditioning, while in the mid-range bracket only some rooms have air conditioning. There are hotels which offer you rooms with air coolers and these work out cheaper and almost as cool as the air-conditioned rooms.

Bills at the top hotels often have to be paid in foreign currency—it is sufficient to change the relevant amount of travellers' cheques with the hotel cashier. Luxury tax, service charges and possibly other taxes may be added.

Travel within Rajasthan

Much of the experience of India is the actual travelling between A and B. It is not always fun, rather it can be extremely frustrating. So often the buses and trains are packed with intense humanity which is easily infused by some excitement, and those interminable stops—they rarely seem necessary—

just make the journeys even longer and more tiresome. But by travelling on public transport you see India going through its daily paces, you are dipped into real India for better or for worse. You will make friends, exchange tales and pass through tracts of land where villages are barely aware of modern technology. Try breaking your journey away from the main centres—the 'off the beaten track' is just a stone's throw from the 'beaten track' and the two are centuries apart. And when the grind of travel finally gets too aggravating and tempers begin to fray, then it is time to adopt that wisest dogma, the greatest panacea: Oriental Fatalism, and just sink back and let matters take their own course.

Meeting India

Trains. The Indian Railway system is famous throughout the world for its sheer size (60,000 km of track), its importance to the population (nationwide some 10 million people travel by train each day) and for its steam trains (a legacy of the British Raj and still so important to modern India) which are regarded with great affection by tourists who appreciate they are an endangered species, already extinct for a generation in the West.

Most of Rajasthan's railway track is metre gauge, rather than the broad gauge (1.67 metres) commonly found elsewhere in India. Trains on the metre gauge are narrower, hence more cramped, and do not have the opportunity to go as fast as their counterparts on the broad gauge. All this becomes relevant when choosing your mode of transport. As a rough rule of thumb: in Rajasthan buses are generally more frequent, quicker, go to more places and are more confortable than trains; however, on night journeys opt for a berth on a train rather than take a bus.

Endeavour to take a train and you are immediately sucked into a bureaucratic quagmire—already you are experiencing 'real India'. Trains are heavily patronised and a reservation is advisable—essential if you want a berth—and this should be made at the earliest opportunity as Indians plan their travels way ahead (especially for the holidays) and services

Reservations

are often fully booked weeks in advance.

You buy a ticket at one counter and make a reservation at another. When reserving a berth you fill in a 'Requisition Form', stating your name, sex and age. Furnished with these details the ticket clerk will select your travelling companions in the neighbouring berths; there is a nominal reservation fee, but the queuing is a tedious affair.

Before the train arrives you will find a list displayed on the platform indicating each passenger's carriage number. A further list with the passenger's berth number is stuck on the side of the relevant carriage. Railway rules state that a passenger must claim his reserved place at least ten minutes before the train leaves. Failure to do so entitles the ticket collector to allocate it to someone else.

No reservation? Well, you will probably end up in the mêlée of a second class unreserved carriage—which is especially worth avoiding on a night journey.

There are several short cuts to obtaining a reservation. Most train services set aside a few berths for tourists, so you can ask the station master if he has any free places on the Tourist Quota. If that is full ask about space on the VIP Quota—or any other quota for that matter. Failing that, approach station officials and with persuasive charm, quick wittedness and maybe a bit of baksheesh you may well muddle through to getting yourself a place. For a commission local travel agents will do the leg work for you (ask at the Tourist Office for the names of such companies) and if a well established agent at home is arranging your travels, ask them to get their counterparts in India to make your train reservations and they will have the tickets waiting for you on your arrival.

If you hold a ticket for a journey over 400 km you can break your trip every 200 km (confirm this with the station master at each leg of the voyage). The advantage is that you do not worry about the whole reservation rigmarole whenever you embark on the next stage.

Rail pass

The Indrail Pass allows you unlimited travel on all trains in India for periods of 7, 15, 21, 30, 60 or 90 days. It can be bought at some travel agents at home (ask your local Indian Tourist Office), or at major stations in India, notably at the Railway Tourist Guide, Northern Railway, Baroda House and the Central Reservation Office, Northern Railway, Connaught Place. Both are in New Delhi. You can get a pass for any of the classes and they have to be paid for in US dollars if bought in India.

The pass probably won't be a money saver as it is unlikely that the cost of all your train travel will amount to the price of a pass—especially in Rajasthan where you are likely to take a few bus rides. But, as it is a ticket, you at least avoid one of those lengthy queues and when you wave your pass at the reservation clerk he may look upon you favourably and give you preference on one of the quotas.

As for the trains, it is worth noting that the 'passenger' train services stop at all the small stations and are considerably slower than the 'express' and 'mail' services. The class structure inside the train is quite complex and there are usually variables within the first class and second class compartments.

Class structure

First class compartments have either two-berth coupés or—slightly cheaper—four-berth cabins; the berths are wide and padded and, for a few extra rupees, you can order sheets, pillow and towel from the station master before departure. The cabins have doors which can be locked to give you privacy. There is a wash basin and loo at the end of each carriage.

Second class compartments are open cubicles which are either two-tier or three-tier. In the two-tier the lower berth is designated to sitting passengers—day and night—while the upper berth is for the passenger who has paid the extra to get somewhere to lie down and sleep. In the three-tier everyone has a berth on which to sleep and these are folded up to provide seating during the day. Second class berths are narrow and cramped; in some trains they have a thin layer of padding. The cubicles don't have doors, so there is no privacy. Though each place in the reserved carriages has been carefully allocated it still seems that there is overcrowding. As in first class there is a loo and washbasin in each carriage.

First class is approximately double the price of second class and for the budget conscious traveller the extra perks don't warrant paying the difference.

Fans provide ventilation in both classes; there is also—on a few services at least—an air-conditioned class which again has different permutations of berthing. The air-conditioned carriage is smarter, more modern and more expensive than first class.

Order within chaos

To an outsider the trains and stations may seem utterly chaotic, but the Indian Railway succeeds because underneath there is, in fact, strict order. Take the catering service: on some trains a member of the kitchen staff will rush around the carriages taking your requests for food—thalis, curries or omelettes. Your meal will be prepared at the next main station and brought to you in your compartment. The portions and contents of the dishes are precisely controlled by the railway authorities. Alternatively there are many vendors who wander up and down the platforms at every station and poke their heads through the windows to offer passengers meals, snacks, fruits, sweets, tea, water and numerous other things. Thousands live and shelter in stations, surviving through selling and begging.

Palace on Wheels

The rejuvenation of the glorious days of the maharajas for the benefit of tourists is at its most advanced in Rajasthan. First it was the palace hotels, then came the Palace on Wheels.

The RTDC brought the maharajas' old trains out of moth balls, they spruced up the carriages, put them on the end of a well-oiled locomotive and offered to show off Rajasthan in style. To travel like a maharaja is a good idea, but the price is high and the standard is not up to scratch (however things may change and for up-to-date information contact your local Indian Tourist Office). A drawback for some, a blessing for others, is that passengers are enclosed in a fancy train and brought out in the open only in neat groups to be shepherded around the main sights. You observe India from one vantage, but never really experience her richness.

The Palace on Wheels operates weekly between the beginning of October and the end of March. Bookings, which can be made through your travel agent at home, should be made well in advance. Below is the tour itinerary:

DAY 1: NEW DELHI

A. Dinner at Delhi Cantt Station 20.00 to 22.30
B. Departure 22.45

DAY 2: JAIPUR

A. Breakfast on board
B. Lunch at Rambagh Palace Hotel—originally Royal Palace of the Maharaja of Jaipur
C. Tea and Dinner at Man Singh/Nahargarh—originally royal fort of Jaipur

DAY 3: UDAIPUR

A. Breakfast on board
B. Lunch at Lake Palace Hotel—originally royal palace of the Maharana of Udaipur
C. Evening tea at Nehru Gardens in Fateh Sagar Lake
D. Dinner at Shiv Niwas—originally royal palace of the Maharana of Udaipur

DAY 4: UDAIPUR—JAISALMER

A. Breakfast on board—morning free
B. Lunch, tea and dinner on board

DAY 5: JAISALMER

A. Breakfast and lunch on board
B. Evening tea on board/Tourist Bungalow
C. Dinner at Moomal Tourist Bungalow

DAY 6: JODHPUR

A. Breakfast on board
B. Lunch at Umaid Bhawan Palace Hotel—originally royal palace of the Maharaja of Jodhpur
C. Evening tea and dinner on board

DAY 7: BHARATPUR and AGRA

A. Breakfast at Shanti Kutir in Bharatpur Bird Sanctuary. By coach to Fatehpur Sikri—ghost city founded and deserted by the Mughal Emperor, Akbar the Great
B. Lunch at Clarks Shiraz Agra
C. Tea at Taj Restaurant/on board, Agra
D. Dinner at Mughal Sheraton/on board

DAY 8: NEW DELHI
A. Breakfast on board

NB 1. Provision is made for sightseeing, shopping, cultural entertainment and free time
2. Minor alterations may be made without notice.
3. Timings and places are subject to change.

Buses. Be wary of blindly immersing yourself in the whole Indian railway experience—especially in Rajasthan where there is a competitive and extensive bus network.

Ordinary service . . .

As with the trains it is wise to know your buses. State buses are either 'express' or 'passenger'; their fares are much the same and work out a little more expensive than a second class train ticket. The main difference between the two services is that the passenger bus stops whenever anybody wants to get on or off and, for the average Westerner, such a journey of village hopping rapidly becomes extremely laborious.

Buses are the more favoured mode of transport amongst locals. In Rajasthan the trains run on metre gauge track (see above) and buses tend to offer a quicker and more frequent service, and there is the added bonus that you do not make reservations. Whether this is such a blessing is a moot point. You do not have the time consuming queues of the railway station; instead you have a free for all scrum as passengers besiege the bus on its arrival. Seats and even standing space are earnestly fought over, the losers—though maybe they are the ultimate winners—end up sitting on the roof where it is less cramped and conditions and tempers are cooler (rooftop travelling is officially forbidden).

Tickets are issued just before the departure, which usually means that there is a scramble at the ticket office. To be quick witted is a great advantage and you may deem it necessary to go round to the back door to confront the ticket clerk, or get someone at the front of the queue to buy your ticket and give them a little baksheesh to make it worth their while. They are phasing in the advance purchase of bus tickets which will, hopefully, do away with the ritual struggle for places, but the overcrowding is an inherent part of Indian travel which is unlikely to disappear.

On the more popular routes—such as Delhi-Jaipur—there is a fast expanding network of State

and luxe deluxe buses run by the RTDC, and private buses. They offer passengers reserved seats which can be bought in advance, the reassurance of your own undisputed seat and, on the fanciest services, air conditioning and a Hindi movie on video (a luxury you might wish to have been spared). These buses give you speed, comfort and relatively few of the headaches you normally encounter when securing your seat, but the price of these privileges is about double the fare of the ordinary bus.

The quality of the buses vary. The ordinary State bus can be an old battered rattling tin can or one of the smart new models which local government is gradually introducing. The State deluxe and private buses are modern and usually well maintained.

Safaris. Camel and Jeep safaris out of Jodhpur, Bikaner and Jaisalmer are becoming increasingly popular. Arrangements with the locals can be made on arrival. Ask at the Tourist Office.

Car hire. You don't really hire cars in India in the same way as you do in the West, rather you employ the services of a chauffeur and his car—which is likely to be one of those ubiquitous Ambassadors, the much cherished vehicle styled on the old Austin Cambridge. This is expensive, and to ensure you are getting a fair deal and that your chauffeur and car are reliable, it is worth making your arrangements through the Tourist Office or other dependable agent.

Air travel. Indian Airlines, India's internal airline, operates Boeing 737 services to Jaipur, Jodhpur and Udaipur. The Delhi–Agra–Jaipur Golden Triangle can also be covered by plane. Fares have to be paid

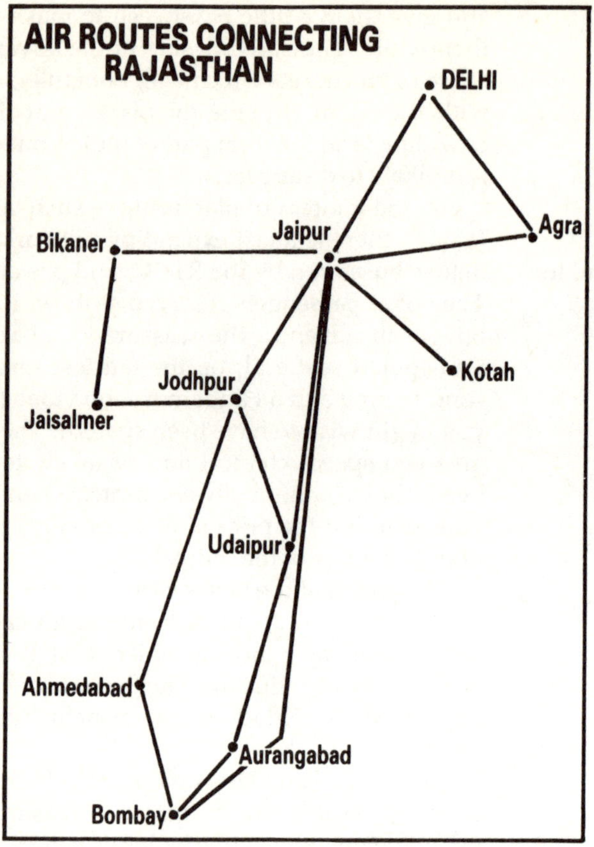

445	493	473	491	IC	Flight Number	IC	492	474	494	446
3,5,7	D	1,4	D		Days		D	1,4	D	3.5.7
	17.40	13.00	06.40	D	Delhi	A	11.35	15.30	22.25	
	18.15		07.15	A	Jaipur	D	11.00	↑	21.50	
20.30	18.45		07.45	D		A	10.30		21.25	20.00
↓	19.25		08.25	A	Jodhpur	D	09.50		20.45	↑
	19.50		08.50	D		A	09.25		20.20	
	↓	14.00	09.25	A	Udaipur	D	08.55	14.30	↑	
			09.50	D		A	08.30			
			10.55	A	Aurangabad	A	07.25			
			11.25	D		D	06.55			
	20.35		↓	A	Ahmedabad	D	↑		19.35	
	21.05			D		A			19.05	
	↓								↑	
22.00	22.00		12.05	A	Bombay	D	06.15		18.10	18.30

The code for days: D = Daily; 1 = Monday; 3 = Wednesday; 4 = Thursday; 5 = Friday; 7 = Sunday.

for in foreign currency and children and people under the age of 30 are eligible for various discounts. Seats on Indian Airlines' services around the country are in great demand, so make your bookings as far in advance as possible and reconfirm your flight two days before departure. Vayudoot Airlines flies from Delhi to Kotah and to Bikaner and Jaisalmer via Jaipur. Ask your travel agent about further details.

Great demand

Transport within towns. In town your choice of transport is likely to be a taxi, an auto-rickshaw, a cycle-rickshaw or, in a few places, a horse-drawn buggy. A fundamental rule applies to all: decide your fare with the driver before embarking on the journey; fail to do so and he may try his luck and demand some hugely exaggerated price at the end. You may get your fingers burnt the first few times, but once you are street wise to the correct prices you should be able to haggle with confidence. The Tourist Office, locals and travellers can give you guidelines about the fares. If there is a meter insist that it is put into use, though the driver may well claim that it is out of order or that the fares indicated are out of date and so on. Make sure that this mutually agreed rate includes the price for carrying your luggage or other passengers. Tipping is not necessary and is a matter of discretion.

Agree the price first

You will find taxis at the railway station at Jaipur and hanging around the up-market hotels in the main cities, but far more common are the rickshaws.

The auto-rickshaw is a three wheeled contraption —a noisy, nippy yellow and black motorised tricycle capable of carrying two passengers. The manual version, the cycle-rickshaw, is cheaper. What a thankless task, peddling around overweight sahibs and memsahibs—especially in the mid-day heat during the hot season. Many of the rickshaw wallahs don't actually own their rickshaws; they rent them from a local entrepreneur for around 10 Rs–20 Rs a day and so it is imperative make a profit.

But best of all hire a bike and do the sweating yourself. When it comes to sightseeing this is often the most practical, convenient and cheapest way of getting around. Bikes can be hired by the hour, day, week or even longer and the day rate, for example, is less than 10 Rs. The Tourist Office will point you in the right direction.

However, when you plan your sightseeing itinerary do consider the coach tours offered by the Tourist Office. They are very good value and are especially worthwhile where the sights are scattered.

Distances Between the Principal Cities

Jaipur to	Agra	230 km
	Ajmer	132 km
	Alwar	143 km
	Bharatpur	176 km
	Bikaner	366 km
	Bundi	207 km
	Chittor	320 km
	Delhi	256 km
	Jodhpur	335 km
	Kotah	245 km
	Mount Abu	491 km
	Sariska	196 km
	Udaipur	435 km
Jodhpur to	Ajmer	203 km
	Bikaner	240 km
	Jaisalmer	287 km
	Mount Abu	265 km
	Udaipur	259 km
Udaipur to	Ajmer	303 km
	Bundi	271 km
	Chittor	115 km
	Kotah	284 km
	Mount Abu	320 km

A Rajasthani beauty

Museums

Rajasthan's history echoes within the walls of its forts and palaces which stand as dignified memorials of the illustrious past. These are museums in themselves. Some have been neglected and lie empty and ghostly, some have now been converted into palace hotels, while others are open to the public and display the finest local riches which will give you an idea of how the Rajput used to behave on and off the battlefield.

You will find palace museums at most of Rajputana's former princely capitals. At best they have been left as they were when they were occupied—restored where necessary and exhibiting the full opulence of the old royalty. Inevitably there are armouries with never ending collections of swords, daggers, armour, guns—so much is beautifully crafted, revealing a brighter side of battle. Fabulous costumes, rugs, exquisite paintings, priceless jewellery, crystal, luxurious decor and furnishings dating from the medieval period to a more modern time confirm the Rajputs' taste for the lavish. The erstwhile maharaja, surrounded by pomp, ceremony and untold wealth, really was as romantic and as exotic a figure as you had hoped for.

A taste for the lavish

Most of the bigger towns also have government museums. Here you will find the remainder of royal families' heirlooms and memorabilia which have not been put in the palace museums. Also they have a greater variety of exhibits—fossils, local archaeological finds, the art, artefacts, costumes and musical instruments of the neighbouring tribes and anything else from the region which the curator deems is of cultural interest. Many of the museums need a bit of brightening up; nevertheless there is something quite endearing about their dusty, rambling and nonchalant state.

Both palace museums and government museums are open daily, except possibly on national holidays and on Fridays or Mondays.

Markets

There can be few greater pleasures than aimlessly wandering the streets of an ancient town or city of the Orient. Try and afford yourself the luxury however tight you are on time.

You will come across markets wherever you go in Rajasthan. You are immersed in a profusion of colours, noises, smells and people which will leave you with all your senses tingling. The huge array of spices, the piles of fruit and vegetables, the freshly made sweets, the leatherwork, the pottery, the gorgeously bright materials, intricately crafted gold and silverware and other splendid jewellery—all are commonplace to the local but exotic to the Westerner. Stroll around, browse, have a chat and take a tea and snack in one of the small cafés.

Regional crafts

Each region of India has its own specialities of handicrafts and those you find in Rajasthan are amongst the most colourful and most popular anywhere in the country.

Bandhani is an old method of tie-dying cloth which is still commonly practised throughout Rajasthan and Gujarat and many of the cholis (blouses), saris, dupattas (veils) and ghagras (skirts) worn by the women have been decorated by this technique.

At Sanganer, near Jaipur, block printing materials is a well established cottage industry, and at Bagru—also not far from Jaipur—the famous local design on cloths is circular patterns. These traditional textile handicrafts now share their market with screen printed fabrics and other factory produced materials.

Meenakari is the highly delicate and intricate decorative art of enamalling gold and silver, and the most skilled craftsmen are found in Jaipur and north of Udaipur at Nathdwara. Locals say that the Kuchwaha Raja Man Singh introduced five enamel workers from Lahore to his capital at Amber in the 16th C. When Sawai Jai Singh built Jaipur the meenakaars moved shop to the new capital and now their descendants are still here continuing their families' centuries old craft business.

Lacquered and engraved brassware have become popular souvenirs, as have the lovely painted papier mache boxes which originate in Kashmir but can be found in emporiums in large towns throughout India.

Mochis, cobblers, will make Western styled shoes to order, but are understandably most adept at producing the mojadis, the local type of slipper, usually made of camel leather and frequently fancily decorated. In the shops you will find shelves full of wallets, belts, sandals, bags and anything else that can be made out of leather.

Buy a length of material and take it to one of the roadside tailors, come back in an hour or two and he will have made up for you a pair of trousers, a shirt or whatever. Away from the boutiques Western fashions in India are still in the 1960s, so specify exactly the style you wish, or else you may end up with flares wide enough to sweep a road or shirt collars which are bound to be too short or too long. Ideally bring along a garment of your own which the tailor can copy, and order it a bit larger to allow for shrinkage after wash (NB the colours in most of the textiles are not fast).

Rajasthan is famous for its schools of miniature painting which have excelled at different periods in different regions. Artists still produce the scenes depicting the favourite tales from mythology and legend. Some of the work is very fine and Udaipur is a centre for the pichwai, or cloth, paintings.

Durries—an Indian style of rug—and carpets are a speciality in Jaipur. Nearby Sanganer, the block printing town, is also a centre for pottery—mostly it is painted with floral patterns in traditional blues and greens. Jodhpur gave its name to the design of riding breeches, though today you will be hard pushed to find a tailor here who can make you a pair. Instead Jodhpur is well known for its puppets and wood carvers.

Wooden articles are mass produced in several places, but you will still come across craftsmen who patiently carve in wood—and stone—the filigreed patterns they learnt from their forefathers.

Marble quarried at Makrana, about 100 km west of Jaipur, was used to build the Taj Mahal and the Victoria Memorial at Calcutta. The marble continues to be exploited and besides being used for practical purposes it is crafted into an assortment of souvenirs. Semi-precious and precious stones are also found in Rajasthan, and they are made into anything from paper weights to the lovely traditionally designed—and also modern styled—jewellery you see in the shops.

Caveat emptor

There is no shortage of antiques for sale. Some are genuine but others are just treated to make them look old. In the better established emporiums (ask the Tourist Office for details) the authenticity of a piece is guaranteed. Here the price will be fixed and fair and this serves as a good guideline before you go down to the bazaar and start bargaining for a similar article.

'Where to buy what' requires a bit of personal research, but ask a local and he will point you in the right direction. Be wary, though, of lads who offer to show you to their 'brother's' or 'uncle's' workshop, they will certainly be earning for themselves a commission for anything you buy and, naturally, this is added onto the price of your purchase.

Festivals

Fabulous festivals, full of colour, noise, smells and happiness, are celebrated by Hindus in honour of the gods and heroes who feature in their ancient mythology. Most follow the lunar calendar and so they fall on different dates each year.

In addition to the important festivals which are celebrated in grand style nationwide, there are numerous smaller fetes held in villages and towns in veneration of a local worthy or diety. Often it is just good fortune that you stumble across festivities in full swing, but it is worth asking the tourist officer and other locals about any impending celebrations in their district—even a typical Hindu wedding procession is fun to see.

All around Rajasthan cattle and camel fairs are held. The largest and most famous is the *Pushkar Mela*, just outside Ajmer, which has become particularly popular with tourists.

Nowadays the RTDC organises special festivals for tourists. The best known is the *Desert Festival* at Jaisalmer—a recent winner of the 'Moustache

Competition' kept his moustache coiled up like a liquorice wheel and when unravelled it stretched 1.5 metres either side of his nose! They can be entertaining—you see well performed and colourful folk dances and music shows, pageantary, camel races and side events portraying local culture —but they lack the true essence and passion of an age old religious ceremony.

Nationwide Hindu festivals

Diwali, the Hindus' equivalent of Christmas and New Year rolled into one and lasting several days during October/November, commemorates the occasion Rama and Sita returned from exile to their capital Ayodhya. Diwali is sometimes called the 'Festival of Lights' because devotees light small oil lamps—usually they set them afloat—to show the couple the way home. Lakshmi, goddess of wealth, is also honoured because it is hoped that she will bring prosperity to the family in the new year. It is a time for exchanging best wishes and possibly gifts.

Holi is, quite literally, the most colourful Hindu festival. It falls in March and celebrates the advent of Spring. The night before, bonfires are lit to destroy the demon Holika and on the day itself people take to the streets armed with coloured paints and powders and—all in good humour—they pelt each other. The Holi celebrations are the closest to a carnival atmosphere you are likely to find in India.

Gangaur starts the day after Holi and lasts 18 days. It is essentially a women's festival in honour of Shiva (Gan) and his consort Parvati (Gaur) who are the personifications of nuptial harmony. Unmarried girls pray for suitable husbands and married women hope to be blessed with long and happy marriages. Traditionally this is when women decorate their hands and feet with mehndi (henna); widows are not allowed to participate in the celebrations. Tod recorded Gangaur: 'The rituals commence, when the sun enters Aries, with a deputation to a spot beyond the city to bring earth for the image of Gauri. When this is formed, a smaller one of Iswara is made, and they are placed together. A small trench is then excavated in which barley is sown; the ground is irrigated till the grain germinates, when the females join hands and dance around it. After that, apparently, the young corn is plucked and presented by the women to the men who wear it in their turbans'. The festival culminates with models of Shiva and Parvati being taken at the head of a procession down to a lake for a ritual bath.

Teej, the 'swing festival' held in July/August, is another occasion dedicated to Parvati and it is celebrated by women to commemorate the day when the queen was reunited with her husband Shiva after a period of isolation. Brothers give their sisters presents—including special saris—and the girls and women play on swings and generally have a good time; they may also decorate their palms and soles with henna.

Raksha Bandhan, commonly called Rakhi, is a touching ritual concerning fraternal duty. A girl will tie a rakhi, usually an ornate string bracelet, around her brother's wrist and by doing so she reinforces the sibling bond and asks her brother for protection. She repeats the procedure every August.

Dushera, one of the great Hindu festivals, spans ten days in September/October and enacts the battle in the Ramayana when Rama defeated the tyrannical demon king Ravana. On the final day bonfires are lit and effigies of Ravana and his accomplices are set ablaze. The event symbolises the victory of good over evil.

Festivals to watch for in Rajasthan

Below are some of the smaller or more localised festivals which are celebrated in Rajasthan:

Baneshwar is a festival celebrated by the tribal Bhil community. It is held at Baneshwar in Dungarpur district south of Udaipur in January/February.

Banganga fair celebrates events recorded in the Mahabharata which took place at this spot near Bairat, northeast of Jaipur, in April/May.

Galiyakot Urs is a festival celebrated by the Bohra Moslems in honour of the 12th C saint Seydi Fakhruddin. It is held at Galiyakot in Dungarpur district south of Udaipur on the 27th day of Moharrum, the first month of the Islamic calendar.

Janmashtami, the festival celebrating the birth of Krishna, is held throughout India. In Rajasthan it is celebrated in greatest style at Nathdwara (north of Udaipur) and Kishangarh (northeast of Ajmer). It falls in August/September.

Jameshwar, a festival of the Bishnoi community in honour of Jameshwari, the founder of their sect, is held near Nokha, southeast of Bikaner, twice a year in February/March and in September/October.

Karni Mata festival commemorates Karni Mata, a 15th C woman who had supernatural powers. It is held at Deshnok, south of Bikaner.

Keladevi, the festival of the goddess Kela Devi, is held at Kelan Devi, northeast of Sawai Madhopur and not far from Karauli, in March/April.

Kolayat celebrates the saint Kapil Muni who lived by Lake Kolayat, southwest of Bikaner, and it attracts thousands of pilgrims in November who believe a dip in the lake will absolve them of their sins. A cattle fair is held at the same time.

Mahaveerji is a Jain festival attracting pilgrims to Mahaveerji in Sawai Madhopur in March/April.

Nag Panchami, the occasion when Hindus nationwide pay homage to snakes and more particularly Sesha (sometimes known as Anant), the thousand-headed mythological serpent which is associated with the god Vishnu, falls in August and is best celebrated at Mandore, just outside Jodhpur.

Ramdeoji, or Ram Shah Pil, was a 15th C saint believed by many to be a reincarnation of Krishna. He preached equality amongst religions and the ten-day festival in his honour, which falls in August/September, draws pilgrims of all faiths to the town of Ramdeoji, just north of Pokaran and east of Jaisalmer. Apparently Ramdeoji loved horses and devotees make him offerings of model horses.

Rani Sati festival honours Narain Devi, who in 1595 was the first of 13 women in her family to commit sati, and is held twice a year in Jhunjhunu in Shekavati district.

Shitala Ashmati, a traditional village festival to Shitala, goddess of smallpox, is held all over India in March/April. The main celebrations in Rajasthan are at Seel ki Doongri near Jaipur. It is also known as the festival of the Bullock Carts and many locals arrive in colourfully painted bullock carts.

Shiv Rati, the festival of Lord Shiva at Eklingji, north of Udaipur, is held in February/March.

Sitabari is a fair celebrated at the place where Sita was left by Laxman near Kelwara, southwest of Shahbad and east of Kotah. The water here is said to cure mental illness.

Urs Mela, a huge festival in honour of Moinuddin Chisti, is held annually in Ajmer; it is the most important Moslem event in Rajasthan.

Veerpuri, the festival held to honour the old heroes of Marwar, is held at Mandore, Jodhpur, in July/August.

Cattle fairs

Some of the cattle fairs held around Rajasthan:

Chandra Bhaga fair at Jhalarapatan, Jhalawar district south of Kotah, is held in November/December.

Gogamedi, a fair in honour of Gogaji, an 11th C Chauhan chief, near Nohar in Ganganagar district northeast of Bikaner, is held in August/September.

Gomatisagar fair is held at Jhalarapatan, Jhalawar district south of Kotah, in May.

Jaswant fair is held at Bharatpur in September/October.

Merta fair is held at Merta, northeast of Jodhpur, in April/May.

Nagaur holds one of the largest and most spectacular cattle fairs in Rajasthan in January/February. The RTDC provides tent accommodation for tourists; alternatively there are places to stay at Nagaur, Bikaner 110 km to the northwest and Jodhpur 135 km to the southwest.

Nimbo ka Nath Mela is a horse fair held at Nimbo ka Nath, near Bali in Pali district northwest of Udaipur, in February/March.

Pushkar Mela, held in October/November just outside Ajmer, is the biggest cattle fair in Rajasthan.

Sanchore, in Jalor district southwest Rajasthan, holds a cattle fair in April/May.

Shiv Ratri cattle fair is held near Karauli, northeast of Sawai Madhopur, in February/March.

Tejaji is a cattle fair held at Parvastar, northeast of Ajmer, in August/September.

Tilwara, one of Rajasthan's more important cattle fairs, commemorates Mallinath, a Rajput hero, and is held at Tilwara, near Balotra in Barmer district and southwest of Jodhpur. It is celebrated in March/April.

Tourist festivals

Inspired by the increase of tourists into Rajasthan the RTDC are laying on more and more *tourist festivals*. At present they are hosted at Jaisalmer (February), Udaipur (April), Mount Abu (June), Jodhpur (October) and Bikaner (November), Jaipur holds various events, including elephant fairs and polo festivals. More such shows will probably follow.

Public Holidays

Here is a list of the main holidays:
New Year's Day
26 January (Republic Day)
Good Friday
Easter Monday
Idul Fitr (June)
15 August (Independence Day)
Janamashtami (August/September)
2 October (Mahatma Gandhi's Birthday)
Dushera (September/October)
Diwali (October/November)
Christmas Day
Boxing Day (26 December)

The religious holidays (Christmas excepted) fall on different days each year. You can find out the dates of the main ones in advance from the Overseas Trade Division, Department of Trade and Industry, 1 Victoria Street, London SW1H 0ET.

Game Parks

The Royal Rajputs, like all good Hindus, would worship a pantheon of animal dieties in their temples, yet at the same time their favourite sport was shooting the game which prowled their lands. Hunting is now banned, and it is ironic that the maharajas' very hunting grounds have been converted into sanctuaries for the creatures they used to prey upon.

Tigers and water birds

Rajasthan has two tiger sanctuaries, the Sariska and the Sawai Madhopur Wildlife Sanctuaries; both are part of 'Project Tiger', an organisation affiliated to the World Wildlife Fund. Another major sanctuary is the Keoladeo Ghana Bird Sanctuary, India's best known water bird sanctuary. Below is a list of Rajasthan's game parks and wildlife sanctuaries.

Bhensrod Garh Sanctuary
Chittor district

Darrah Sanctuary
Kotah district

Desert National Park
Jaisalmer district

Dhawa Sanctuary
Jodhpur district

Gajner Sanctuary
Bikaner district

Gavial National Sanctuary
Kotah district

Jaisamand Sanctuary
Udaipur district

Keoladeo Ghana Bird Sanctuary Bharatpur district

Kumbhalgarh Sanctuary
Udaipur district

Mount Abu Sanctuary
Mount Abu district

Sariska Wildlife Sanctuary
Alwar district

Sawai Madhopur Wildlife Sanctuary
Between Jaipur and Kotah

Sitamata Sanctuary
Udaipur district

Tal Chhaper Sanctuary
Bikaner district

Van Vahir and Ram Sagar Sanctuaries
South of Agra

The standard and availability of accommodation varies from place to place. You may be able to chose from a palace hotel and a Tourist Bungalow or, at the more obscure sanctuaries, there may only be a simple DAK Bungalow or Rest House or even nowhere to stay at all. Entry prices into the sanctuaries are also variable (you may have to pay an extra 'camera fee' if you take photos) and a guide may be obligatory. It would be wise to contact the Tourist Office at the nearest main town to find out about transport to the sanctuary, the accommodation situation, what facilities are available once you get there and any quirky seasonal opening times.

Accommodation at the parks

A Rajasthan Itinerary

The Golden Triangle

You must incorporate the 'Golden Triangle'—Delhi-Agra-Jaipur—somewhere in your itinerary. Preferably take a train from Delhi to Agra, ideally the Taj Express which leaves New Delhi daily at 07.05 and arrives at Agra three hours later.

Agra is the home of the Taj Mahal, the white marble mausoleum built by the Mughal Emperor Shah Jahan in the 17th C for his favourite wife Arjumand Banu, who was better known as Mumtaz Mahal—the 'chosen one for the palace'. Shah Jahan was usurped by his son Aurangzeb and the aging emperor was confined to Agra's Red Fort from where, they say, he spent his final days gazing across the River Yamuna at the tomb of his beloved wife. The Taj Express returns to Delhi in the evening and so it is quite feasible to make Agra and a visit to the Taj Mahal a day's outing from the capital. Enroute you pass through **Mathura**, birthplace of Krishna, and hence an important place of pilgrimage.

40 km west of Agra is **Fatehpur Sikri**, capital of the Mughal Empire between 1570 and 1586. Emperor Akbar built this splendid city, but later it was abandoned because of the poor water supplies. Today Fatehpur Sikri remains deserted, but it is still intact, a marvellous relic of the golden days of the Mughal Empire.

Continuing west you enter the state of Rajasthan at **Bharatpur**, a city famous for its fabulous water bird sanctuary and its lovely pleasure palaces just to the north at **Deeg**. Eventually you reach Jaipur, 230 km west from Agra by road.

Jaipur, the Pink City, was created in the 18th C

by Sawai Jai Singh, the inspired maharaja of the Kuchwaha Rajput clan, and soon it developed into the most prosperous city in Rajputana. After Independence Jaipur was chosen as the capital of Rajasthan and today it is also the state's main tourist centre.

Excellent bus services run frequently from Jaipur back to Delhi; alternatively take one of the daily trains—the Pink City Express, the Delhi Express, the Chetak Express or the Delhi Mail—though they will take a bit longer. However, you may wish to make a detour and stop off at the **Sariska Tiger Sanctuary** or the palace city of **Alwar**. Or you can take a more circuitous and westerly route back to Delhi, by bus or train, via **Jhunjhunu** and the region of **Shekavati**, which is fast becoming popular because of its wonderfully painted havelis.

Jaipur gateway

But hopefully you will have time to penetrate deeper into Rajasthan, and Jaipur serves as the gateway for further exploration.

Remaining in eastern Rajasthan you can take a train or bus southwest to **Ajmer**, former capital of the Chauhan Rajputs and one of Rajasthan's oldest and most historic cities. Today the tomb of Mohud-din Chisti, a 13th C Moslem saint, attracts over 100,000 pilgrims on the occasion of the annual Urs Mela festival. A huge cattle fair is held at nearby **Pushkar** each year.

Continuing south by road or rail you will pass through lovely and richly historic hills dappled with remarkable monuments like the 15th C **Kumbhalgarh** fort, the **Ranakpur** Jain Temples, the **Nathdwara** Krishna Temple and the **Eklingji** Shiva Temple; here too is **Haldigathi**, the most famous battlefield on which Rajputs stood against the Mughals in defence of their lands. Then you come to **Udaipur**, founded in the 16th C as the new capital of the princely state of Mewar; it is one of the most exotic cities in India. The Lake Palace, now a hotel, rises from the centre of Lake Pichola and on the banks there is the vast and beautiful City Palace.

Udaipur palaces

Go west by bus from Udaipur to Abu Road and then up the windy path to **Mount Abu**, the only hill station in Rajasthan and a cool sanctuary from the plains during the hot summers. Or go east to **Chittorgarh**, the old capital of Mewar, an awesome fort which remains an honoured symbol to the courage of the Sisodia clan, who from these battlements fought more heroically than any to keep out the invading Moslems.

Ajmer is directly north of Chittorgarh and is easily reached by train or bus. Or if you push further east by bus you pass by **Mandalgarh**, another great 15th C fort, and the ancient temple complex at **Bijolia** before you reach the delightful palace city of **Bundi** which, though little visited by tourists, boasts one of the finest palaces in Rajasthan. Its sister town of **Kotah** on the banks of the River Chambal, 36 km to the south, has become industrialised, but it has a good museum and is well known for the old Kotah school of miniature paintings.

Kotah is on the main Bombay-Delhi broad gauge railway line. On your way back to Delhi you can break your journey at **Sawai Madhopur**, where you will find another tiger sanctuary and the decaying fort of **Ranthambore**. A branch line also links Sawai Madhopur with Jaipur to the northwest.

Cities of the Thar Desert

West of Jaipur lies the Thar. The desert and the three major desert cities—Jaisalmer, Jodhpur and Bikaner—offer a different experience to eastern Rajasthan.

The road northwest from Jaipur skirts western Shekavati before turning directly west for **Bikaner**. The train journey involves changes, but if you plan to go direct from Delhi to Bikaner you can always take the Bikaner Mail by night or the Bikaner Express by day. Bikaner was founded by a branch of the Rathores in the 15th C and owes much of its development this century to the enterprise of Maharaja Ganga Singh. Though interesting, Bikaner is not as special as either Jodhpur or Jaisalmer.

There are trains from Delhi (including the 10-hour Super Fast Express), Jaipur, Bikaner and Udaipur to **Jodhpur**—famous to the outside world for its riding breeches—but known in India as the capital of the Marwar Rathores and for its dramatic Meharangarh fort which so splendidly crowns the city.

Remote corner of India

It is 300-odd dusty km by train (you can go by bus or take a camel) from Jodhpur to **Jaisalmer** near the Pakistan border, and it is probably wisest to cover the monotonous tracts by night train from Jodhpur. As you approach early the next morning you see in the distance this ancient walled honey coloured city slowly rising out of the dull flat sands. This is as remote and fascinating a city as you are likely to find in India.

DELHI AND AGRA

Though neither Delhi nor Agra are in Rajasthan, no trip to northwestern India would be complete without a visit to these two cities. Indeed, along with Jaipur, Rajasthan's capital, they constitute the spectacular 'Golden Triangle', the most thoroughly trodden tourist path in India. Below is a brief introduction to Delhi and Agra.

Delhi's Seven Cities

They say that Delhi comprises seven ancient cities, built by successive ruling dynasties. Their remains exist in different states of repair, lying scattered around present Delhi.

Hindu founders, Moslem conquerors

The Chauhan Rajputs ruled the region from **Qila Raipithora** (Delhi's first city), which lies south of modern Delhi. They were overthrown in the late 12th C by the Moslems, who went on to establish the Delhi Sultanate. Qutb-ud-din Aibak, the first sultan and founder of the Slave or Mamluk dynasty, destroyed 27 Hindu and Jain temples and then undertook his own building programme. He constructed the **Quwwat-ul-Islam (Might of Islam) Masjid**, the first mosque on Indian soil and **Qutb Minar**, a remarkable 72.5-metre tower; both monuments still stand and are amongst Delhi's major sights today. There is a 2000-year-old *iron pillar* in the complex; with your back against it, encircle it with your hands and your wishes in life will be granted.

Alaudin invaded India and won Delhi at the end of the 13th C. He supplanted the previous dynasty with his own Khilji line and created **Siri** (the second city), his own capital, northeast of Qila Raipithora; its large reservoir, **Hauz Khan**, lies just to its west.

The Tughluqs followed the Khiljis in 1321 and the first in the dynasty, Ghiyasuddin, founded the huge fortified 13-gate **Tughluqabad** (the third city)

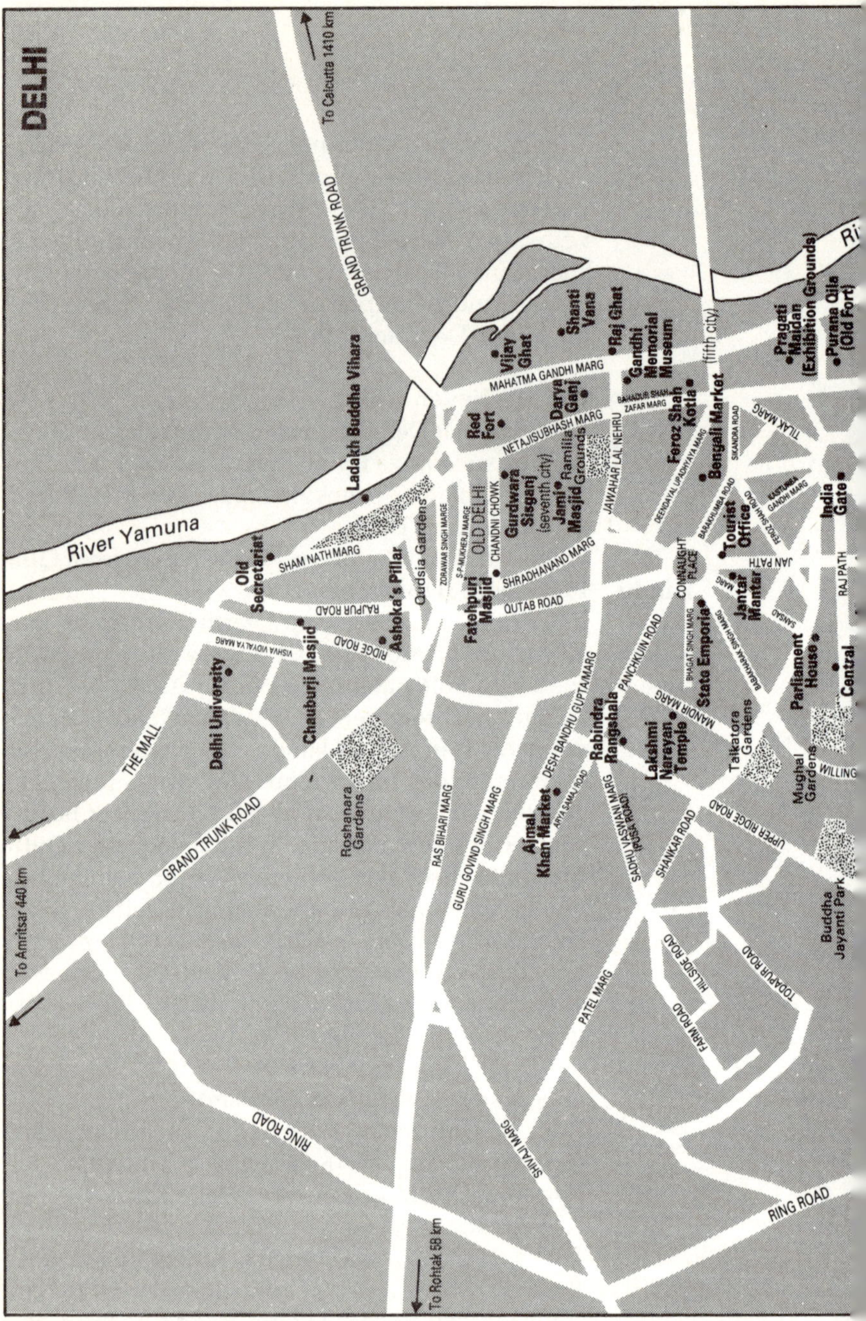
DELHI
River Yamuna
To Calcutta 1410 km
GRAND TRUNK ROAD
Ladakh Buddha Vihara
Old Secretariat
SHAM NATH MARG
RAJPUR ROAD
RIDGE ROAD
Ashoka's Pillar
Qudsia Gardens
VISHVA VIDYALYA MARG
Delhi University
Chauburji Masjid
THE MALL
Roshanara Gardens
To Amritsar 440 km
Red Fort
NETAJISUBHASH MARG
MAHATMA GANDHI MARG
Vijay Ghat
Shanti Vana
Raj Ghat
Gandhi Memorial Museum
Darya Ganj
BAHADUR SHAH ZAFAR MARG
OLD DELHI
CHANDNI CHOWK
Gurdwara Sisganj
(seventh city)
Jami Masjid
Ramlila Grounds
JAWAHAR LAL NEHRU
Feroz Shah Kotla
Bengali Market
(fifth city)
Pragati Maidan (Exhibition Grounds)
Purana Qila (Old Fort)
Fatehpuri Masjid
SHRADHANAND MARG
QUTAB ROAD
CONNAUGHT PLACE
Tourist Office
Jantar Mantar
JAN PATH
State Emporia
BHAGAT SINGH MARG
PANCHKUIN ROAD
India Gate
TILAK MARG
SIKANDRA ROAD
RAJ PATH
Parliament House
Central
MANDIR MARG
Lakshmi Narayan Temple
Taikatora Gardens
Mughal Gardens
WILLING
Rabindra Rangshala
DESH BANDHU GUPTA MARG
Ajmal Khan Market
ARYA SAMAJ ROAD
RAS BIHARI MARG
GURU GOVIND SINGH MARG
SADHU VASWANI MARG (PUSA ROAD)
SHANKAR ROAD
UPPER RIDGE ROAD
Buddha Jayanti Park
HILLSIDE ROAD
TODAPUR ROAD
FARM ROAD
PATEL MARG
SHIVAJI MARG
RING ROAD
To Rohtak 58 km

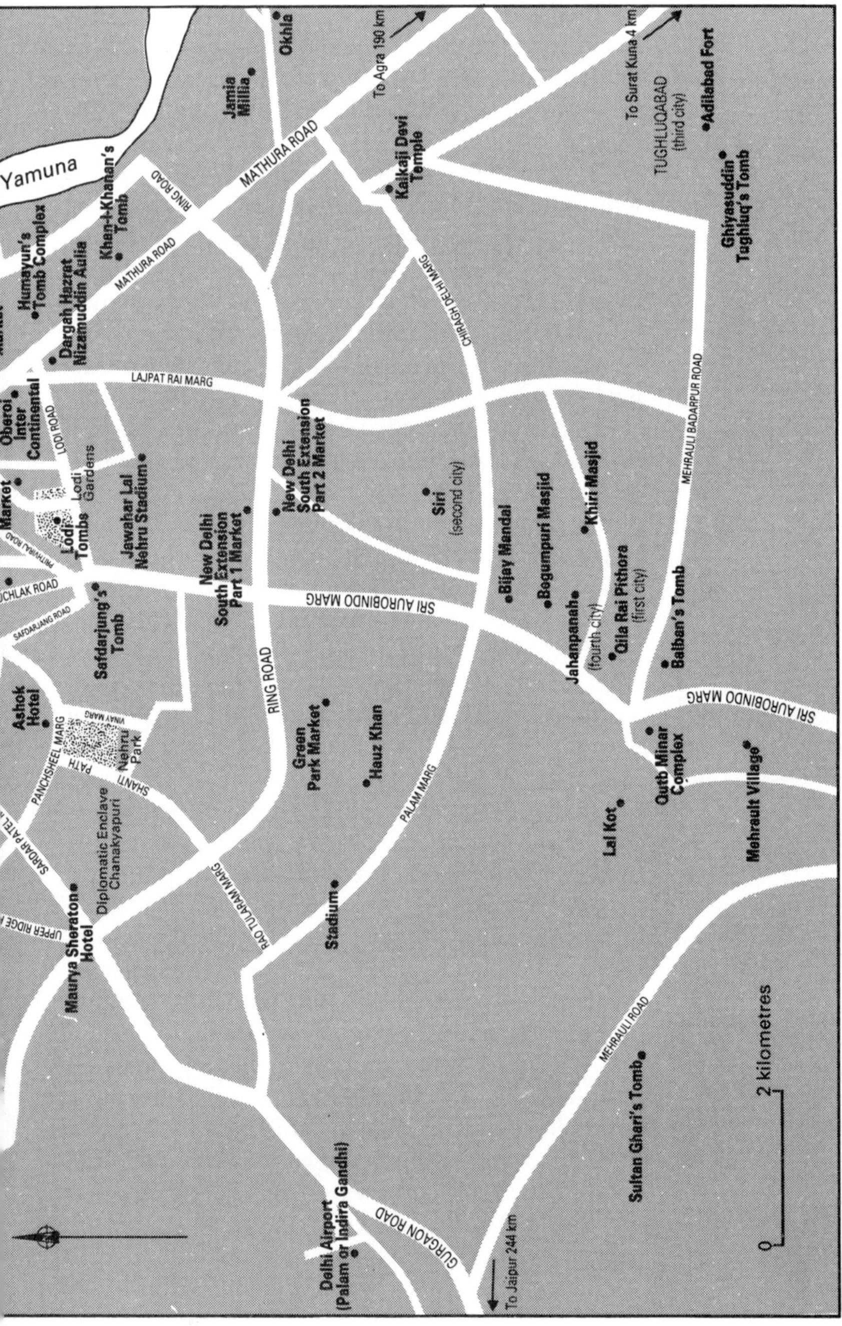

Yamuna
Okhla
Jamia Millia
To Agra 190 km
MATHURA ROAD
RING ROAD
Humayun's Tomb Complex
Khan-i-Khanan's Tomb
Dargah Hazrat Nizamuddin Aulia
Kalkaji Devi Temple
To Surat Kund 4 km
TUGHLUQABAD (third city)
Adilabad Fort
Ghiyasuddin Tughluq's Tomb
LAJPAT RAI MARG
LODI ROAD
Oberoi Inter Continental
Lodi Gardens
Lodi Tombs
Jawahar Lal Nehru Stadium
New Delhi South Extension Part 2 Market
New Delhi South Extension Part 1 Market
CHIRAGH DELHI MARG
Siri (second city)
MEHRAULI BADARPUR ROAD
Bijay Mandal
Begumpuri Masjid
Khiri Masjid
Qila Rai Pithora (first city)
Jahanpanah (fourth city)
Balban's Tomb
SRI AUROBINDO MARG
PRITHVIRAJ ROAD
SAFDARJANG ROAD
Safdarjung's Tomb
Ashok Hotel
VINAY MARG
PANCHSHEEL MARG
SHANTI PATH
Nehru Park
Diplomatic Enclave Chanakyapuri
SARDAR PATEL
UPPER RIDGE
Maurya Sheraton Hotel
Green Park Market
Hauz Khan
PALAM MARG
RAO TULARAM MARG
Stadium
Qutb Minar Complex
Lal Kot
Mehrauli Village
MEHRAULI ROAD
Sultan Ghari's Tomb
2 kilometres
0
Delhi Airport (Palam or Indira Gandhi)
GURGAON ROAD
To Jaipur 244 km

southeast of Siri. South of Tughluqabad are the remains of the 10th C **Suraj Kund**, a large Rajput amphitheatre. And to the north there is an inscription carved in rock by the Emperor Ashoka (273–36 BC).

Rajput amphitheatre

Ghiyasuddin was killed by his son Muhammad who went on to build **Jahanpanah** (the fourth city), just east of the ancient Rajput Qila Raipithora. However, Tughluqabad continued as capital, though Muhammad did try to resettle his entire population down in Maharashtra, and when that proved to be unsuccessful he brought them all the way back again.

Feroz Shah succeeded Muhammad in 1351 and he built an expansive capital, **Ferozabad** (the fifth city), with its core further north along the banks of the Yamuna. Important here is the 3rd C **Ashoka Pillar** inscribed with Ashoka's edicts for peace. Nearby is **Mahatma Gandhi's memorial**.

After the Tughluqs came the Sayyid (1414–44) and Lodi (1451–1526) dynasties. Neither built new cities, but are famous for the tombs they left behind. And these still stand in the **Lodi Gardens** (present New Delhi). In fact this little district is rich in mausoleums: the **Safdar Jang tomb** (Safdar Jang was prime minister to an 18th C Mughal emperor) is one of the last classic Mughal garden tombs. At the other end of Lodi Road is **Hazrat Nizamuddin**, a medieval district which grew up around the tomb of Nizamuddin, a highly revered 13th C Moslem saint; other famous people are also buried here in the dargah. Across the Mathura Road is the **Mughal Emperor Humayun's magnificent tomb**.

Garden tombs

Barbur swept into India and, having defeated Ibrahim Lodi, he founded the Mughal dynasty. Fourteen years later Sher Shah usurped the Mughal throne, destroyed Emperor Humayun's fledgling city of Dinpanah and on its ashes he constructed the formidable **Purana Qila** (the sixth city). It is believed that a settlement had existed on this site some 3000 years ago. Opposite is the mid-16th C mosque, **Khairul Manazil Masjid**; just to the south is the **zoo**, the best in India, and beyond you see Humayun's tomb.

Akbar and Jahangir—and Shah Jahan during the early years of his reign—chose Agra as their official seat. In 1638 Shah Jahan returned to Delhi to found his new capital near old Ferozabad. Unlike the earlier cities **Shahjahanabad** (the seventh city) is today very much a living city. This is **Old Delhi**, a true city of the Orient: pick your way through the tight alleys and narrow lanes to get a feel of India and wander the length of the wide and busy **Chandni Chowk**—it was once the richest bazaar in the East and it remains a lively and colourful market. Visit the **Jami Masjid** (built between 1644 and 1658), the largest mosque in India, and the immense **Red Fort** (Lal Qila) which was commenced in 1638. A sound and light show is staged in the evenings at the fort.

A living city of the old Orient

New Delhi: Modern British and Indian Capital

As rulers of India the British initially governed their colony from Calcutta. In 1911 George V, King of England and Emperor of India, proclaimed the transfer of the capital to Delhi. Edwin Lutyens and his team of architects set to work and south of Shahjahanabad they created the grandoise **New Delhi**, which was officially inaugurated on 9 February 1931.

At the core of British Delhi stands **India Gate**, commemorating soldiers of the Indian Army who died in wars during the early years of this century. Straight wide avenues radiate in neat patterns from here across spacious midans. It is all well ordered and symmetrical. The main Rajpath leads west to the immense imposing **Rashtrapati Bhavan**, built on Raisini Hill as the viceroy's residence and now occupied by India's president. Here too is the **Sansad Bhavan**, the Parliament.

Raj grandiosity

Just to the south is the equally uniform **Chanakyapuri enclave**, where rows of elegant mansions occupied by the world's diplomats stand surrounded by manicured lawns and well trimmed hedges. The identity of each is recognisable by its flag and highly polished plaque on the gate. Nearby is the city's race course and then further south stretch the residential suburbs, often parcelled into what are locally referred to as 'colonies'. Unlike say Bombay, Delhi has had land in which to expand.

Walk north of Rajpath along Janpath. To the left down Tolstoy Marg is the **Jantar Mantar**, one of Jai Singh's outdoor observatories. Continue along Janpath and you pass the small souvenir shops which line the final stretch before Connaught Place.

Connaught Place, a series of concentric circular roads, is the city's commercial hub. This is where you will find the greatest concentration of shops, offices, banks, travel and booking agencies, airline offices, national and state tourist offices, restaurants and so forth. It is a prime site, being on the border of Old and New Delhi and in the centre of the city as a whole.

Delhi's centre

Delhi has many museums; consult local guide books or the Tourist Office for full details. The following two museums are of particular note: the **National Museum** (Janpath, south of Rajpath) houses a rich collection of historic Indian art and archaeological finds; the **Nehru Museum** (Teen Murti Road, near Chanakyapuri) was the residence of Jawaharlal Nehru, India's first prime minister, and is now open to the public.

Agra: Flower of Shah Jahan

Having won the Battle of Panipat in 1526, Barbur went on to occupy the Lodi's city of **Agra**. The earliest Mughals initiated few buildings and it was under Akbar—who moved his capital here from Delhi—that Agra began to blossom. Jahangir embellished the city further, but it was during Shah Jahan's reign that Agra flowered, reaching its most sublime state with his construction of the Taj Mahal.

The **Taj Mahal** is a testimony to the Mughals' dedication to beauty and perfection—and to love (to please the romantics), for the Taj is a mausoleum

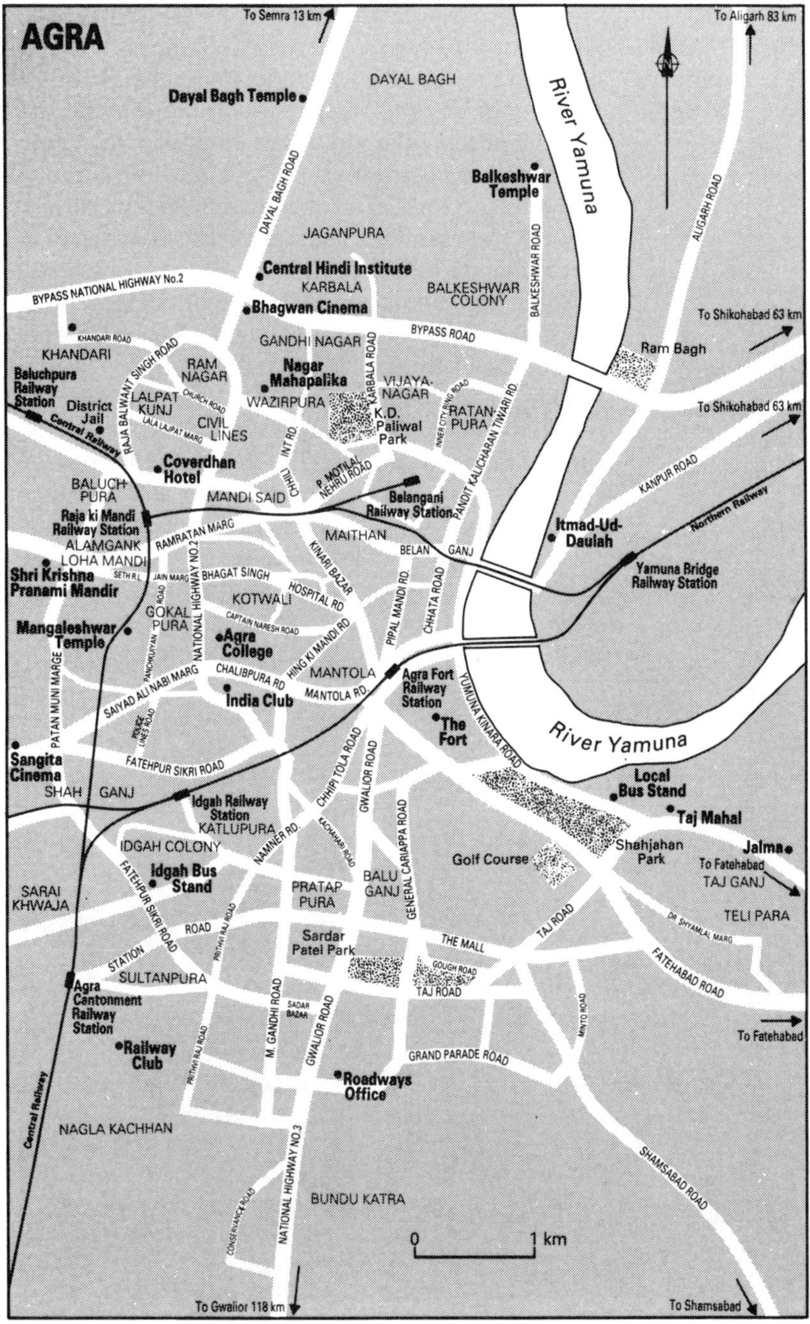
AGRA
To Semra 13 km
To Aligarh 83 km
DAYAL BAGH
Dayal Bagh Temple
River Yamuna
Balkeshwar Temple
DAYAL BAGH ROAD
ALIGARH ROAD
JAGANPURA
BALKESHWAR ROAD
Central Hindi Institute
KARBALA
BALKESHWAR COLONY
BYPASS NATIONAL HIGHWAY No.2
Bhagwan Cinema
To Shikohabad 63 km
KHANDARI ROAD
GANDHI NAGAR
BYPASS ROAD
Ram Bagh
KHANDARI
RAJA BALWANT SINGH ROAD
RAM NAGAR
KARBALA ROAD
Nagar Mahapalika
VIJAYA-NAGAR
Baluchpura Railway Station
CHURCH ROAD
LALPAT KUNJ
WAZIRPURA
INNER CITY RING ROAD
RATAN-PURA
PANDIT KALICHARAN TIWARI RD.
District Jail
LALA LAJPAT MARG
CIVIL LINES
K.D. Paliwal Park
To Shikohabad 63 km
Central Railway
INT RD.
Coverdhan Hotel
P. MOTILAL NEHRU ROAD
KANPUR ROAD
BALUCH-PURA
MANDI SAID
CHHILI
Belangani Railway Station
Northern Railway
Raja ki Mandi Railway Station
RAMRATAN MARG
MAITHAN
Itmad-Ud-Daulah
ALAMGANK
BELAN GANJ
LOHA MANDI
KINARI BAZAR
Yamuna Bridge Railway Station
Shri Krishna Pranami Mandir
SETH R.L.
JAIN MARG
BHAGAT SINGH
HOSPITAL RD
PIPAL MANDI RD.
CHHATA ROAD
KOTWALI
GOKAL PURA
CAPTAIN NARESH ROAD
Mangaleshwar Temple
Agra College
NATIONAL HIGHWAY NO.2
HING KI MANDI RD
PANCHKUIYAN ROAD
CHALIBPURA RD
MANTOLA
Agra Fort Railway Station
SAIYAD ALI NABI MARG
MANTOLA RD.
India Club
YUMUNA KINARA ROAD
The Fort
PATAN MUNI MARGE
POLICE LINES ROAD
River Yamuna
Sangita Cinema
FATEHPUR SIKRI ROAD
CHHIPI TOLA ROAD
GWALIOR ROAD
Local Bus Stand
SHAH GANJ
Idgah Railway Station
Taj Mahal
KATLUPURA
KACHAHARI ROAD
GENERAL CARIAPPA ROAD
NAMNER RD.
IDGAH COLONY
Shahjahan Park
Jalma
Golf Course
To Fatehabad
SARAI KHWAJA
FATEHPUR SIKRI ROAD
Idgah Bus Stand
BALU GANJ
PRATAP PURA
TAJ GANJ
TELI PARA
ROAD
PRITHVI RAJ ROAD
DR SHYAMLAL MARG
Sardar Patel Park
THE MALL
TAJ ROAD
STATION
SULTANPURA
GOUGH ROAD
FATEHABAD ROAD
Agra Cantonment Railway Station
M. GANDHI ROAD
SADAR BAZAR
GWALIOR ROAD
TAJ ROAD
MINTO ROAD
To Fatehabad
Railway Club
PRITHVI RAJ ROAD
GRAND PARADE ROAD
Roadways Office
Central Railway
NAGLA KACHHAN
NATIONAL HIGHWAY NO.3
SHAMSABAD ROAD
BUNDU KATRA
CONSERVANCE ROAD
0
1 km
To Gwalior 118 km
To Shamsabad

built by Shah Jahan for Mumtaz, his favourite wife.

The Taj Mahal: symbol of India

As one of the finest structures of all time anywhere on earth the Taj—a godsend to any tourist board—became an obvious symbol to promote India. So alluring is the Taj and so successful was the campaign, that now they advertise that 'there is more to India than the Taj' in a bid to diffuse the tourists around the country. The Taj is the showpiece at the vanguard—the vast nation beyond is as rich as any with magnificent art and architecture.

Agra is the bottom right point of the 'Golden Triangle'—Delhi lies 204 km to the north and Jaipur 230 km to the west. Agra is an easy day trip by rail from Delhi and this is best achieved by taking the Taj Express. But the Taj—let alone the rest of Agra—deserves more than a fleeting and perfunctory excursion. The Taj is best visited at dawn when the light is most mellow and the crowds have yet to arrive; the Taj dazzling under the full moon draws tens of thousands. Being a Moslem monument, the Taj is particularly popular on Fridays.

The Taj Mahal at Agra

Along a meander in the River Yamuna lies the large and historic **Red Fort**, built by Akbar in 1570. You can see the Taj from here and legend claims that Shah Jahan, imprisoned in the fort by his son Aurangzeb, spent his final days gazing at the white marble sepulchre which entombed his beloved Mumtaz.

Akbar's mausoleum, 10 km from the fort at **Scindia**, is worth a trip. But most important after the Taj is a visit to the lovely 17th C **Itmad-ud-Daulah's Tomb**, which is the other side of the river, about 2 km from the fort.

It takes five hours by bus to Jaipur via Bharatpur. It is worth, however, making a slight detour to visit the marvellous though now deserted **Fatehpur Sikri**, Akbar's capital between 1570 and 1586. Fatehpur Sikri is 40 km west of Agra and 27 km southeast of Bharatpur.

PRACTICAL INFORMATION

DELHI

New Delhi, India's capital, is one of the main international gateways into the country and a convenient starting point for a venture into Rajasthan.

Arriving and departing by plane

Palam (or Indira Gandhi), Delhi's **airport**, is 17 km southwest of the city. A seemingly endless queue of **taxis** await bumper-to-bumper for newly arrived passengers. It appears to be quite common practice for the taxi driver to overcharge his fare, so—if the meter 'doesn't work'—it is advisable to determine the cost of the ride beforehand. The **tourist and hotel desks** in the airport will give you relevant information; there is also an **exchange counter** where you can change money.

Much cheaper than the taxi is the convenient EATS; Ex-Servicemen's Air Link Transport Service. The old **buses** provide a reliable and fairly regular service from the airport into Connaught Place, the heart of Delhi, and they will drop you off at hotels on the way. Going in the other direction, the bus leaves from the south side of Connaught Place for the airport every hour or two between 04.40 and 23.30.

Remember, you have to pay an **airport tax** when departing on international flights.

Where to stay

Delhi—comprising Old and New Delhi—is a sprawling city and you may want to choose your hotel according to its location. Some years ago there was a spate of hotel construction and the most luxurious accommodation was built along the spacious and leafy residential avenues of New Delhi—especially around the Chanakyapuri diplomatic enclave—between the airport and Connaught Place.

Delhi's **top hotels** are:

Hotel Ashok, 50-B Chanakyapuri, New Delhi 110021; tel: 600121; telex: 031-2567; managing group: ITDC (the hotel is the flagship of the government run Ashok chain of hotels); rooms: 589. Built in the 1950s the Ashok for a long time enjoyed an unrivalled position as Delhi's only modern deluxe hotel. To keep in stride with the more recent and flashier competition (i.e. the five hotels listed below) the Ashok has undergone a dramatic facelift—which has included repainting its characteristic pink exterior white.

Hyatt Regency, Bhikaji Cama Place; tel: 609911; managing group: Hyatt Hotels; rooms: 550.

Maurya Sheraton, Sardar Patel Marg, New Delhi 110021; tel: 370271; telex: 031-3247/4911 WELC IN; managing group: Welcomgroup Hotels; rooms: 510.

Oberoi Intercontinental, Dr Zakir Hussain Road, New Delhi 110003; tel: 699571; telex: 2372/3829 OBDL; managing group: Oberoi; rooms: 330.

Taj Mahal Hotel, 1 Mansingh Road, New Delhi 100011; tel: 386162; telex: 31-3604/31-4758 TAJD IN; managing group: Taj Hotels; rooms: 350.

Taj Palace Hotel, Sardar Patel Marg, New Delhi 110021; tel: 344900; telex: 031–5151 TAJD IN; managing group: Taj Hotels; rooms: 500.

The above half-dozen hotels are large, modern and of the ultimate deluxe category. They have all the mod cons, facilities, restaurants, bars, nightclubs (these tend to be Delhi's most up-market and popular night spots) and shopping arcades that you would expect to find in top international hotels anywhere in the world. Rooms cost 1000 Rs for a double, give or take 100 Rs or so. Be prepared to take taxis for trips in and out of town.

In the same area of town is the colonial *Claridges* (12 Aurangzeb Road, New Delhi 110011; tel: 370211; telex: 031 2518; rooms: 140)—ever popular with those who hark back to the days of the Raj and who prefer the intimacy and charm of **old-style hotels**. Also built in colonial times and in the characteristic design of that era is the *Imperial* (Janpath, New Delhi 110001; tel: 311511; telex: 3303 HTL IMP; rooms: 160), which has an excellent downtown location just off Connaught Place; it is the best of the cluster of hotels in Janpath. Both Claridges and the

Imperial have five stars and are about 40% less expensive than the deluxe hotels.

Another fine colonial hotel with character is the turn of the century *Oberoi Maidens* (Alipur Road, Delhi 110054; tel: 2525464; telex: 2703 OMDL; rooms: 75), which is the other side of town on the northern edge of Old Delhi and thus convenient for the bazaars and sights of Shahjahanabad rather than for New Delhi. It is a four-star and a little less expensive than the above two hotels.

There is **budget accommodation** in Old and New Delhi and the most convenient quarter to stay—at least to start off with—is around Connaught Place. The large one-star government-run *Ashok Yatri Niwas* (Ashok Road, Janpath; tel: 344511) is comparatively clean, well equipped and inexpensive (double rooms range from about 100 Rs to 250 Rs). If it is full or not suitable the staff or the nearby Tourist Office will point you towards smaller, even more moderately priced lodges in the area.

Sightseeing

The Government of India Tourist Office and the Delhi Tourism Corporation (see below for addresses) can also provide you with information about **city sightseeing tours** and **out of town excursions** and they will give you **brochures and maps** of Delhi. There are many locally and foreign-published guide books on Delhi as a whole and on the various individual sights; they are readily available from bookstalls and many are very inexpensive. The weekly *Delhi Diary* gives background information on the city, useful addresses and a 'what's on' guide to the events of the week.

Useful addresses

Foreign embassies and high commissions:

Australia, 1/50-G Shantipath; tel: 601336.

Britain, Shantipath; tel: 601371.

Canada, 7/8 Shantipath; tel: 608161.

France, 2 Aurangzeb Road; tel: 374682.

Germany (West), 6/60-G Shantipath; tel: 604861.

USA, Shantipath; tel: 600651.

Air travel:

Aeroflot, Kanchenjunga Building, Barakhamba Road; tel: 42843 (392331, airport).

Air France, 6 Scindia House, Janpath; tel: 604691 (392730, airport).

Air India, Scindia House, Janpath; tel: 344225 (392621, airport).

British Airways, 1-A Connaught Place; tel: 343428 (293111, airport).

Indian Airlines, Kanchenjunga Building, Barakhamba Road; tel: 40084-86 (393544-47, airport).

KLM, 106 Surya Kiran, Kasturba Marg; tel: 351786 (393481, airport).

Lufthansa, 56 Janpath; tel: 343234 (392336, airport).

Pan Am, Chandralok, 36 Janpath; tel: 345344 (392283, airport).

Thai International, 12-A Connaught Place; tel: 343608 (392526, airport).

Palam Airport, tel: 393481.

Information:

Delhi Tourism Corporation, N Block, Connaught Place; tel: 46356.

Government of India Tourist Office, 88 Janpath; tel: 320005.

Rajasthan Tourist Development Corporation, Chandralok Building, 36 Janpath; tel: 322332.

On to Rajasthan

It is worth dropping in on the **RTDC** (see above for address) for full details of transport into Rajasthan, brochures, accommodation information and so on.

There are daily Indian Airlines **flights** to Jaipur, Jodhpur and Udaipur.

Day and night **train services** operate to points all around Rajasthan. Realise that there are two main stations: Delhi Station is in Old Delhi, near the Red Fort, and most of the Rajasthan services leave from here, New Delhi Station—where you catch the train to Agra—is to the north of Connaught Place.

A reservation for a sleeping berth on a train is essential. The easiest way to get one is by visiting the Indian Railways Headquarters, Baroda House, Kasturba Gandhi Marg (near India Gate, with its entrance in Copernicus Road) where they will put you on the Tourist Quota; having done that you should be able to claim your reservation at the railway station. They will explain the exact procedure at Baroda House—or ask the Tourist Office or RTDC. First class and air-conditioned class reservations can be made at the Northern Railway Reservation Office, State Entry Road, Connaught Place. Indrail Passes are obtainable at these two places.

There are also many **bus services** into Rajasthan and, to Jaipur anyway, they tend to be a more convenient and faster means of transport than the train services. Deluxe buses leave for Jaipur every hour between 06.45 and 17.30 from Bikaner House, near India Gate in New Delhi. A little cheaper, though less comfortable, are the ordinary buses which operate regularly from the Inter State Bus Terminal (ISBT), near Kashmiri Gate just north of Delhi Station. Services from here continue up to 23.30; some deluxe buses also leave from the ISBT. It is safer to make a reservation in advance, though it is not as essential as on the trains.

AGRA

There is a fair choice of **accommodation** in Agra. Top of the list is the excellent *Mughal Sheraton;* second is the *Clarks Shiraz.* The mid-range and modest hotels tend to be 2 to 3 km from the Taj amongst the cluster of streets on the way to Agra Cantonment Railway Station—convenient if you arrive from Delhi by train. Or you can find a cheap—possibly far from salubrious—bed in the alleys opposite the Taj Mahal itself.

Hiring a bike and cycling around is the best way to see Agra.

THE JAIPUR REGION

The Hawa Mahal at Jaipur

The Kuchwahas rose from obscurity to a prominent position amongst the Rajput clans after establishing an early bond with Akbar. Such an action was, of course, totally despised by the fervent nationalists such as the Sisodias who felt the Kuchwahas had sold their soul for self-betterment. Indeed Rana Pratap, the Sisodia ruler, came into direct conflict with Man Singh (heir to the Kuchwaha throne and senior general in Akbar's army) at the Battle of Haldighati. The breaking down of barriers between the Kuchwahas and the Mughals had, though, set a fine example. With peace came prosperity and the free flow of ideas, trade and art. Exposure to a wider world benefited the Kuchwahas and under Jai Singh, their canny and erudite statesman-king, their new capital of Jaipur became the modern thinking and cosmopolitan city in Rajputana. And today Jaipur remains Rajasthan's capital and most advanced city.

The Kuchwahas of Dhundar

Having overthrown the Meena tribe in the 11th C, the Dhola Rae dynasty of Kuchwahas controlled the region of Dhundar from their capital at Amber (6 km from present-day Jaipur). However, their rise to prominence amongst the Rajput clans came later, after they had forged an alliance with the Mughals.

In 1561 Raja Bharmal met Akbar at Deosa—between Ajmer and Agra—and offered the emperor his daughter in marriage and through this union Salim, later Emperor Jahangir, was born.

Rise of the Kuchwahas

With the family bond established the Kuchwahas now began to appear in the Mughal court. By the time Man Singh—nephew of Akbar through marriage—ascended the Kuchwaha gaadi in 1590 he had already proved himself as an outstanding soldier in the Mughal army. He was the 'most conspicuous of all the generals of the Empire. To him Akbar was indebted for half his triumphs' (Tod).

As a favourite of the emperor, Man Singh was able to consolidate a strong position for himself, and though the relationship eventually grew sour—Akbar tried to kill Man Singh with poisoned sweets, but he himself unwittingly ate the doctored portions and died—he did, nevertheless, maintain a reasonably high profile in Rajputana.

Man Singh died in 1614 and the next ruler of substance was Mirza Jai Singh (1621–1667), who excelled in Aurangzeb's army and courted friendship with the Mughals. But it was not until the reign of Sawai Jai Singh that the princely state of Dhundar reached its zenith: 'The Cuchwaha state, as well as its capital, owes everything to Jai Singh: before his time it had little political weight beyond that which was acquired from the personal character of its princes and their estimation at the Mughal Court' (Tod).

Zenith of the princely state of Dhundar

When Jai Singh was presented to the Imperial Court at the age of nine, Aurangzeb was so impressed by the lad's repartee that he gave him the epithet 'Sawai', meaning one and a quarter, because he forecast he would be one and a quarter times as great as Mirza Jai Singh.

Sawai Jai Singh ascended the throne four years later in 1700. Ahead of him lay a remarkable reign of forty-three years. He and the emperors had their differences, but on the whole the affinity between the Kuchwahas and the Mughals which had developed over the last 150 years remained intact and benefited both parties.

Jai Singh skilfully steered his state through the troubled times of the early 18th C when the Mughal Empire began to disintegrate, but, while he was a fine statesman and one of the most outstanding men of his time, he was not the archetypal dashing Rajput: 'His courage', wrote Tod, 'had none of the fire which is requisite to make a Rajput hero; though his talents for civil government and court intrigue, in which he was the Machiavelli of his day, were at that period far more notable auxiliaries. As a statesman, legislator, and a man of science, the character of Sowae Jey Sing is worthy of ample delineation'.

And so Sawai Jai Singh is remembered for his accomplishments off the battlefield. He was an astronomer and had works by Ptolemy and Euclid translated into Sanskrit. He sent emissaries to study the old observatories in Maragha (built by Tulsi in 1259) and Samarkand (built by Uleg Beg, grandson of Timor, in 1425). Manuel Figueirado, a Jesuit father in Goa, was authorised by the King of Portugal to assist Jai Singh with his research of the cosmos, and the British based at Surat loaned him maps and globes of the universe.

Astronomer prince

Jai Singh built five observatories—known as Jantar Mantars—at Delhi, Jaipur, Mathura, Ujjais and Varanasi. Jaipur's Jantar Mantar was built in 1728—four years after the one at Delhi, but before the completion of Jaipur city—and today this largest masonry observatory in the world stands in a neat garden in the city centre next to the palace. He also compiled the Zij Muhammad Shahi, the celebrated astronomical tables named after the contemporary emperor in Delhi.

'Until Jey Sing's time, the palace of Amber, built by the great Raja Maun (Man Sing), inferior to many private houses in the city, was the chief royal residence. The Mizra Raja (Mirza Jai Singh) made several additions to it, but these were trifles compared with the ediface added by Sowae Jey Sing, which has made the residence of the Cuchwaha princes as celebrated as those of Boondi or Oodipoor, or, to borrow a more appropriate comparison, the Kremlin at Moscow' (Tod).

Jai Singh founds Jaipur

But Jai Singh's wish was to create a new well planned city from scratch and eventually this ambition was realised when, in November 1727, the foundations of Jaipur were laid some 6 km south of Amber.

Jai Singh and Vidyadhar, his brilliant young architect, combined their talents to construct the magnificent Jaipur. The city is divided into nine rectangular sections representing the nine divisions of the universe. The central square is occupied by the palace (City Palace). Eight gates provide access into the city and the main street runs east to west, entering and leaving Jaipur through Chandrapol, Moon Gate, and Surajpol, Sun Gate; another important road runs south–north through the city and continues up to Amber and eventually Delhi.

Jai Singh made his first ceremonial tour of Jaipur six years after its inauguration. It must have been a splendid occasion and the raja had a grand two-tiered, four-elephant-drawn carriage, the Indra Viman, to take him through the streets.

Jai Singh lived in Jaipur for his final 15 years. His successors made their own additions and the city, originally white, was painted its famous pink so as to minimise the harsh reflected glare.

Visiting Jaipur: Capital of Rajasthan

In 1727 Sawai Jai Singh founded **Jaipur** and soon after moved his capital here from the old fortified city of Amber which lies 6 km to the north. Modern Jaipur—Rajasthan's capital, largest city and centre of tourism—now sprawls beyond the original city

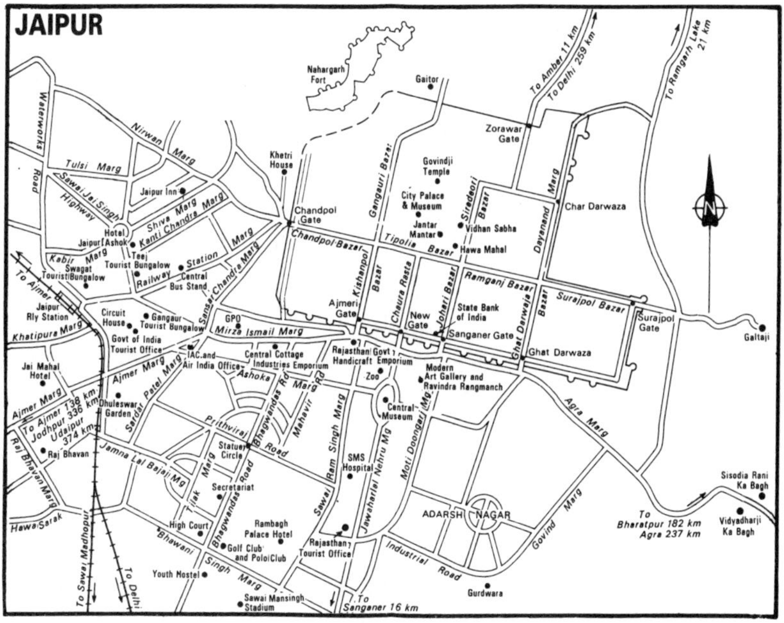

walls, but within the old confines many of the historic buildings and much of the traditional character still exist.

Palace of the maharajas

In the heart of the Pink City is the **City Palace** (1727), the town residence of the maharajas of Jaipur; the present royal family only occupies certain quarters, as most of the palace is now a museum. *Mubarak Mahal*, the Palace of Welcome, stands in the first main courtyard and was built in 1900. Now it is a gallery exhibiting the wardrobes of the former rulers and it includes clothing worn by the immense 2-metres tall 270 kg Madho Singh I, a maharaja celebrated for fathering 100 children. In the *Sileh Khana*, the armoury, across from the Mubarak Mahal, there is a marvellous display of weapons, including arms used by medieval Rajput heroes.

The ornate gateway, *Rajendra Pol*, is flanked by two white marble elephants and, for the benefit of tourists, a couple of palace guards sporting impressive handle-bar moustaches and dressed in full livery, who will pose for the cameras. The gateway leads into a large courtyard in the middle of which is the *Diwan-I-Khas*, formerly an audience and banqueting hall. The weapons on the wall have been arranged in the shape of the sun, as the royal Kuchwahas are Suryavanash, the sun clan of the Rajputs. And the two huge silver urns—apparently the largest crafted silver objects in the world—were filled with holy water from the Ganges and taken by Maharaja Madho Singh II on his trip to Europe earlier this century.

Another gate leads to *Chandra Mahal*, the Moon Palace, the oldest part of the City Palace, with its seven storeys of delicately carved chambers and balconies. On the ground and first floors there are collections of rugs, paintings, sculptures, glassware, jewellery, chandeliers, sculptures and manuscripts; some of maharajas' portraits were painted by a German artist in the 1930s. The four gates to the Pritam Niwas Chowk, the royal winter chamber, represent the four seasons; singing girls used to entertain royal audiences from a balcony above.

Official guides to the City Palace can be found at the main gate. Opening times are 09.30 to 16.45; closed on national holidays.

To the north, Chandra Mahal overlooks a formal Mughal garden. At the far end is the **Temple of Govindji**. Jai Singh saved a Krishna effigy from the blows of the Moslems, intolerant of images, and enshrined it at this spot. Each day priests put Krishna through his daily routine, changing his clothes, etc, and the event attracts many reverent devotees. It is worth popping along to witness one of these sessions: 05.15, 08.15, 10.30, 12.00, 17.15, 18.30 and 20.00. Beyond the temple are other gardens and ponds.

Royal observatory

Opposite the City Palace is the **Jantar Mantar**, created in 1728 and the best of Jai Singh's five observatories. The strange looking structures are precision astronomical instruments able to measure azimuths, altitudes, the distances between the stars and to forecast eclipses. The huge *Samrat* is a sundial with a gnomon (the arm casting the shadow) of 27 metres and the famous *Yantra Raj* is a celestial map. Opening times are 09.00 to 17.00.

The nearby **Hawa Mahal**, Palace of Winds, stands five storeys high and is little more than a facade measuring a metre or two in thickness. Each floor is a row of ornately designed protruding kiosks and balconies; women were able to stand here and look through the finely carved window screens down onto the street without being observed. The Hawa Mahal, built in 1799, was so named because it was designed to allow the breeze to ventilate the interior. You can climb the palace between 10.00 and 17.00.

Palace of the Winds

Around the corner in Tripolia Bazaar is the seven storeyed **Isvar Lat**, the 'minaret piercing heaven', which was built in the 1740s by Sawai Iswari Singh.

Ram Niwas Bagh, a park covering some 30 hectares to the south of the Pink City, was created by Sawai Ram Singh in 1868 to provide work during a time of famine. Within the neat gardens is the curious Oriental-Victorian style Albert Hall, designed by Sir Swinton Jacob in 1887, and which now houses the **Government Central Museum**. In the gloomy interior you will find some interesting exhibits including miniature paintings, portraits of Jaipur's maharajas, handicrafts, ethnographic displays and a section on evolution. Opening times are 10.00 to 17.00; closed on Fridays. Nearby is the **Carpet Museum**. Also in the Ram Niwas Bagh is the **Ravindra Manch theatre** and a small **zoo**—animals include encaged tigers and there is a crocodile and python breeding farm.

Tiger Fort

Nahagarh—Tiger Fort—was built by Sawai Jai Singh in 1734 on top of the hill which rises dramatically above the plain on the northern outskirts of Jaipur. The fort was intended as a possible refuge in the event of an attack on the city, but it became a prison for those who fell out of favour with the royal household. Until recently only the keenest visitors bothered to climb the long, steep, windy path up to the fort. However, the new tarmac road now enables cars and buses to reach the summit. Within the formidable walls there are small palaces which, though deserted, are decorated with typical Rajasthani murals. The views over Jaipur and the plains below are magnificent. Opening times are 10.00 to 16.30.

In the evening shadows of the Nahagarh's hill are the **royal cenotaphs of Gaitor**. Most significant is the finely carved 20-pillared white marble chattri of Sawai Jai Singh and the cenotaphs of Madho Singh (1768), Pratap Singh (1803) and Sawai Ram Singh (1880).

Environs of Jaipur

In a valley 8 km out of town along the Agra road is the **Sisodia Rani-ka-Bagh**—the palace and gardens of the Sisodia queen; on the way you pass the terraced gardens of Vidyadhar, named after Jai Singh's chief architect. Jai Singh married a princess from Mewar (Sisodia clan); however there was friction between the two states and as the rift widened Jaipur's royal household shunned the Sisodia queen. Her son, Madho, was heir to the throne and, anxious for his safety, the queen built her own palace out of town and moved there with the child. Madho eventually inherited his father's position. Opening times are 08.00 to 19.00.

You can continue from Sisodia Rani-ka-Bagh to the pilgrim spot of Galta. Enroute is the **Hanuman temple** where daily at 16.00 a priest summons the wild monkeys for their food. At **Galta**, in a gorge a few kilometres further on, there are temples—the main one being the **Sun Temple**—and pools and springs which locals claim have healing powers. It is a popular picnic spot and is at its most attractive when the hills are greenest after the monsoons.

Sanganer, 12 km south of Jaipur near the airport, is famous for its block printing on textiles and handmade paper and pottery. A large proportion of the inhabitants are involved in this cottage industry.

Amber fort overlooking Lake Moata

The 15th C **Jain temple**, and to a lesser extent the **Krishna temple**, are Sanganer's other attractions.

Journey to Amber

The old Kuchwaha capital

Soon after dawn the sun's early rays fall on the ochre-coloured walls of Amber fort. This is the best time to visit **Amber**, 6 km north of Jaipur. The fort, rising from the steep hill slope, glows in the mellow light and its reflection is perfectly framed in the glass-like surface of Lake Moata below; the stillness of the water is occasionally broken by the bathing elephants and water buffaloes.

Buses leave frequently for Amber from near the Hawa Mahal in Jaipur; taxis and auto-rickshaws are also available, but they can be expensive if the driver waits for you while you tour Amber and then returns you to Jaipur. From the bus stand at Amber you can either walk or take a ride on an elephant up to Amber **fort**. You will find official guides near the entrance.

The Kuchwahas had occupied the site at Amber

for over 500 years before Man Singh founded the fortress palace—previously the main stronghold had been at the hilltop fort of Ramgarh 25 km to the northeast.

Jai Pol, the first gate, leads you into a large courtyard enclosed partly by the old stables, some of which have now been converted into handicraft shops. On the south side two silver doors serve as the entrance to the *Shila Devi temple*. Aartis—prayer sessions—are announced by drum beats at 10.00 and 18.00.

Steps lead up to *Singh Pol*—built by Ram Singh in the 1670s—and the gate opens into another courtyard with Mirza Jai Singh's *Diwan-I-Am*, the hall of audiences, to one side. Quite typically the women, who respected strict purdah, would observe events from up in the galleries and the finely carved screens kept them out of sight from the men below.

The fortress palace

The ornate *Ganesh Pol*—also built during the reign of Mirza Jai Singh—leads to an inner palace. Immediately to the left and right are corridors to various chambers and in the lovely gardens beyond there is the *Sukh Niwas* (Pleasure Palace) with its fountains, water channels and neat lawns and flower beds. Opposite, in the *Jai Mandir* (Hall of Victory) is the *Sheesh Mahal* (an inner chamber) which has been inlaid with thousands of small mirrors. Light a match and you will see it reflected in each of the pieces of glass.

Below Jai Mandir are the marble bathing quarters and above is *Jas Mahal*, a private apartment decorated with inlay work and painted in delicate colours, from where there is a panoramic view over Lake Moata and Amber town. The older sections of the palace lie beyond this courtyard and can still be visited.

Opening times at Amber fort are 09.00 to 16.30.

Amber **town**, below the fort to the west and north, is still inhabited. The **Jagat Shiromani** temple is worth a visit and amongst Amber's **royal cenotaphs** are those of Man Singh (1614), Mirza

Amber's Shiromani Temple

Jai Singh (1667) and Raja Ram Singh (1688), which has carved panels depicting mythological and historical events.

The Mughal-style Dilaram gardens, near the main road, back onto Moata Lake from where you can hire a boat to the Mohan Bari gardens in the middle of the lake. The Amber **archaeological museum**, in the Dilaram gardens, exhibits stone sculptures, pottery and a fine collection of old coins.

On a summit above and to the south of Amber fort is **Jaigarh fort**—Victory fort—which was founded by Man Singh in 1600, though most of it was built by Mirza Jai Singh and his successor Sawai Jai Singh in the late 17th and early 18th C. The large walls cover an impressive circumference, but within there is little to see. There are the remains of the old iron foundry where cannons were made; the immense *Jaivana cannon* can be seen on the other side of the fort. The Jaivana was cast in 1726 during the reign of Sawai Jai Singh, but it was never fired. It is 10.5 metres long and it is believed that had it ever been used it would have taken 60 kilograms of gunpowder to shoot a 60 kilogram missile a remarkable distance of 48 km. The Jaivana weighs over 50,000 kilograms and it required the strength of four elephants to change its direction.

Treasure of Jaigarh

The fort's water resources were channelled from streams in the surrounding hills into three tanks. The largest of these, a huge subterranean reservoir, has a capacity of 67.5 million litres of water and could keep the occupants sufficiently supplied for two years. In 1975 an old document was found which stated that riches had been buried under the tank. The water was drained, but nothing of value was found and this led to the theory that Sawai Jai Singh had used the treasure to finance the construction of Jaipur, his new capital.

Jaigarh was opened to the public in 1983 and you can walk up to it from Amber fort. Opening times are 09.00 to 16.30.

East of Jaipur: Bharatpur

Mewat, the rugged northeast corner of Rajputana, served as a buffer zone between the Mughals in Delhi and the Rajput principalities. The Mewatis were frequently at war with the Mughals—there was a time when the western gates of Delhi had to be barred each evening to keep out their raiding parties—and the Imperial forces were never able to totally suppress them.

The majority of Mewatis were Jats, traditionally a clan of farmers and small landowners, who carved for themselves their own kingdom, exclusive of the Rajputs, with their capital at Bharatpur.

Bharatpur: gateway to Rajasthan from Agra

Bharatpur, the entrance into Rajasthan from Agra and Fatehpur Sikri, was created by the Jats who rose up against Aurangzeb in the late 17th C and later, after the Mughal emperor's death, staked out and consolidated their domains.

The rather drab, busy town has now engulfed the solid remains of **Lohagarh fort** built by Badan Singh early in the 18th C. Erected on flat land and surrounded by a moat, the fort is not one of the most spectacular in Rajasthan, nevertheless the two towers, Jawahar Burj and Fateh Burj, either side of the main gateway commemorate historic victories over the Mughals and the British respectively. Indeed, in the early 19th C the Jats withstood a six-week siege by British troops under the command of Lord Lake.

The palace within the fort walls has been converted into a *museum* housing a dusty collection of the personal effects of past rulers and their families. There are also the archaeological finds which have been excavated from the various local sites. Opening times are 09.00 to 17.00.

But Bharatpur's greatest attraction is the **Keoladeo Ghana bird sanctuary** which was originally founded as a duck shooting preserve by Maharaja Kishan Singh at the beginning of this century. The River Gambir was purposely flooded in the rainy season, leaving large tracts of marshy wetlands, and this proved to be an ideal habitat for many different species of birds. The maharaja invited prominent figures from around the world to hunt on his estate and senior British colonials were amongst his most frequent guests—Lord Curzon was the guest of honour at the first shoot in 1902. There is a rock in the sanctuary on which the old shooting records were etched: The Lord Chelmsford shoot bagged 4206 birds with 50 guns and in 1921 the Prince of Wales shoot claimed 2221 birds.

India's most impressive water bird sanctuary

Keoladeo, named after the Keoladeo Siva temple in the middle of the park, was declared a sanctuary in 1964 and then a national park in 1981. The reserve covers nearly 30 square kilometres and is the most impressive water bird sanctuary in India. Huge numbers of birds migrate to Keoladeo from all over Asia each winter, often breeding here before flying off when the weather warms up. A boatman will take you out on a punt or you can walk or cycle around the sanctuary (best time is dawn and dusk). There is also a dawn minibus tour which leaves from the tourist bungalow. Amongst the 360 or so species of birds, you will see various herons (Keoladeo is one of the best heronries in the world), egrets, cormorants, darters, storks, cranes—including the saras crane, the world's tallest flying bird and the rare Siberian crane (December–January)—geese, ducks, moorhens and flamingoes. A full list of birds is available at the park entrance. The best season to visit Keoladeo is between September/October and February when most of the migratory birds fly in to breed; relatively few species remain behind for the summer.

Deeg: Idyllic Refuge

While Bharatpur was the Jats' capital, the **pleasure palaces of Deeg**, 32 km to the northwest, served as an idyllic refuge for the maharajas. Suraj Mal, Badan Singh's successor, developed the then modest complex at Deeg but was killed before he could complete his delightful retreat.

Various palaces enclose a neat Mughal-style garden, *Gopal Bhawan*, the largest palace, has an

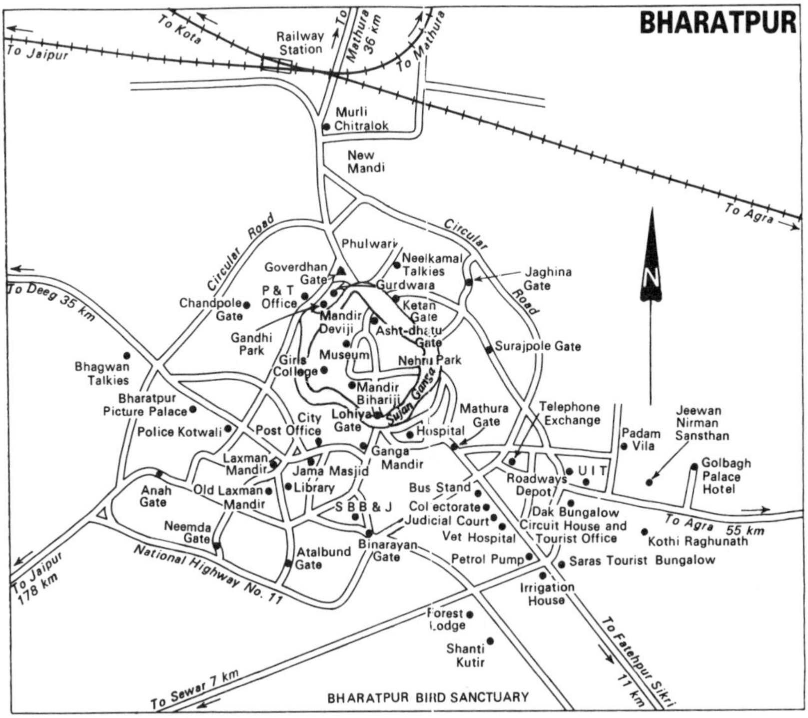

impressive banquet hall and dining room and is flanked by the Sawon and Bhadon pavilions, which are notable for their curved Bengali roofs.

In 1762 Suraj Mal had the audacity to attack the Red Fort in Delhi and the plunder he brought back to Deeg included a section of the white marble Suraj Mahal and a swing Emperor Jahangir had once given to his wife.

Bettered only by the Taj Mahal

The prize party piece at Deeg was the 500 small fountains. Partly fed by a water reservoir on the roof of Kishan Bhawan, the fountains were turned on to create the effect of the monsoon; colourful objects lodged by the nozzles reflected an array of bright shades in the spouting jets and cannon balls were rolled along an underground gutter to simulate the noise of thunder.

Locals will tell you that Deeg's enchantment is

bettered only by the Taj Mahal. Deeg was chosen as the set for *Siddartha*, the film based on Herman Hesse's famous novel.

Northeast of Jaipur: Alwar

Nestled in a valley amongst the Aravalli hills with its once formidable fort dramatically crowning one of the peaks, **Alwar** was of strategic importance and the Kuchwaha Rajputs, Jats, Mughals and the Marathas all fought for the city and each held sway over it at different periods.

The palace complex, the **Vinay Vilas**, on the edge of Alwar was founded as recently as the late 18th C by Bakhtawar Singh and was completed in 1927 by Raja Jai Singh. Most of the palace has now been converted into offices for local civil servants, and in the large courtyard below, rows of typists, clicking away on their antiquated machines, offer to type letters and documents for their fellow citizens.

The upper floors of the palace are now occupied by one of Rajasthan's better *museums*. There are the usual displays of archaeological finds, memorabilia from the royal household and weaponry, including the swords of Emperors Akbar and

Stuffed waiter

Jahangir—and amongst the stuffed animals there is a black bear which used to act as waiter until he lost his temper with one of the guests and had to be put down. Of particular interest is the fabulous collection of miniature paintings and rare Arabic and Persian manuscripts; more curious are the grains of rice which have been microscopically inscribed with messages or verses from the Koran.

Opening times are 10.00 to 17.00; closed on Fridays and national holidays.

Behind the palace wide flights of steps lead down to the large **Sagar tank** and small red marble pavilions protrude into the water at regular gaps. On one side is the *cenotaph of Bakhtawar Singh* which was built in 1815 and is unusual because of its Bengali-style arches and roof.

Sagar tank has a lovely setting. Behind, the barren hills rise sharply and you can see the remains of the **fort walls**, 11 km in circumference, which were impressively built on the steep slopes. On the way up are the relics of Salim Mahal where Salim, later Emperor Jahangir, was imprisoned by his father, Akbar, for dabbling in court intrigue and plotting the assassination of Abul Fazl, an influential advisor to the emperor. By foot it is a long and wearying ascent up to the **fort**—it is possible to make the journey by jeep—and permission to enter the fort must be obtained beforehand from the police down in town. Inside there are the ruins of the *Nikumbh Mahal* (palace of the Rajput Nikumbh dynasty) and various temples and pools. The panoramic views from the battlements over the valleys are spectacular.

Down by the railway the **tomb of Fateh Jung**, one of Shah Jahan's ministers, indicates the Mughals' presence in Alwar; but the tomb is interesting mainly for its fusion of Hindu and Islamic styles of architecture.

At present the ex-royal family live in **Vijay Man-**

The City Palace complex at Sagar Tank, Alwar

dir Palace, 10 km out of town, which was built in the 1920s. The splendid **hunting lodge** built by Vinay Singh for his queen in 1845 overlooks Lake Siliserh 13 km from Alwar and is now the pleasant government-run Lake Castle Hotel. This is a good picnic spot and you can take a boat out and go fishing.

The remains of **Bairath**, to the west of Alwar on the road to Jaipur, date back thousands of years and they feature in the great ancient Hindu epic, the *Mahabharata*. The Mauryans occupied Bairath in the 3rd C BC during the reign of Asoka, a convert to Buddhism and one of India's most inspired leaders of all times. Bairath flourished as a Buddhist centre and you can still see some of the relics of the old Buddhist monastery.

Saving the Tiger

On the way from Alwar to Sariska a shrine marks the place where Bharathari, a local king, retired to live the life of an ascetic having repudiated all worldly values.

Sariska Tiger Reserve, 37 km southwest of Alwar on the road to Jaipur, is one of the main reasons why tourists pass through Alwar. In 1978 the reserve, covering a vast region of forested hills and valleys and with a core area of 500 sq km and a total area of 800 sq km, became part of 'Project Tiger'. The project has met with success and in the last ten years the number of tigers has increased from 11 to over 30.

Encompassed within the reserve are 20 or so villages—the inhabitants are mainly agriculturists herding cattle—and a host of historic sites, including the ruins of old Shaivite and Jain temples, the site of Garh Rajore, an 8th to 10th C settlement, and the deteriorated Kankwari fort where Aurangzeb imprisoned his younger brother Darah Shikoh.

From big cats to birdlife

Sariska is the home for a variety of animals besides the tiger. There are small numbers of leopards and panthers, but much more common are the different species of deer, such as the chital

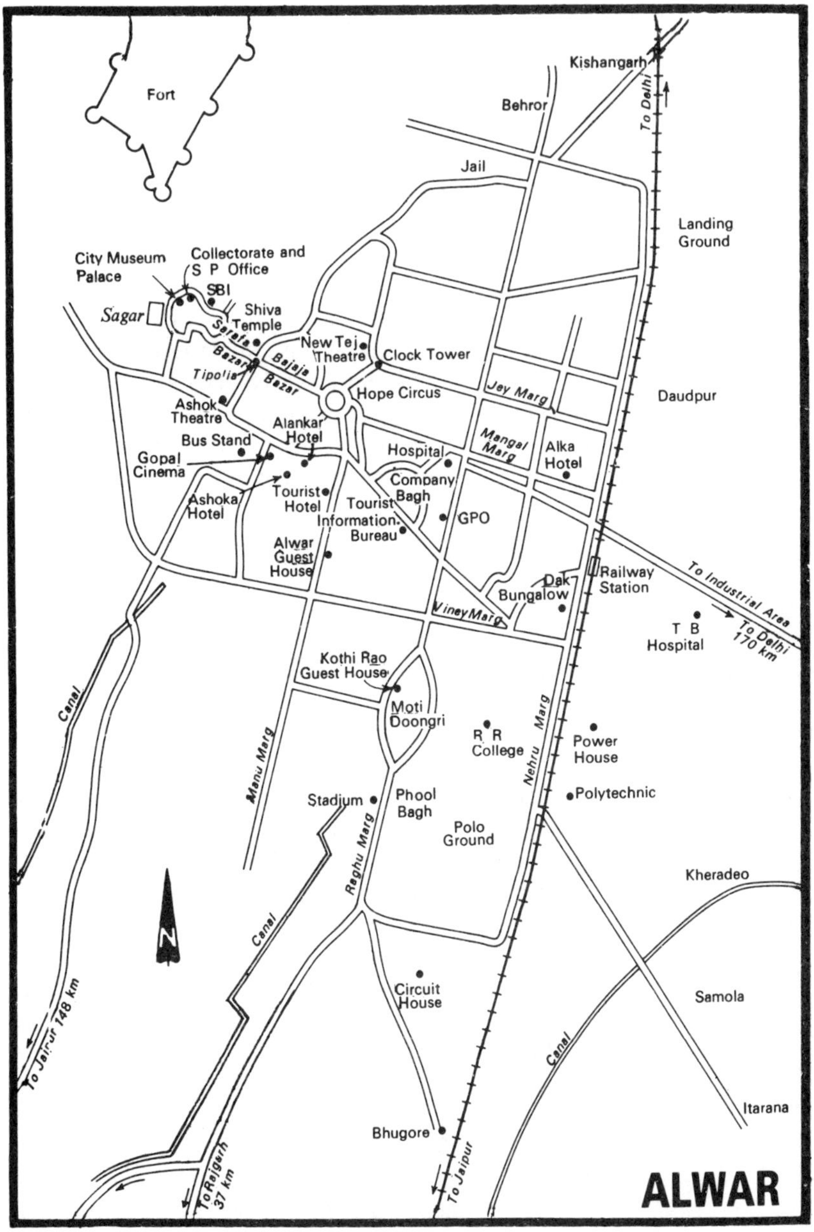
ALWAR
Fort
Kishangarh
To Delhi
Behror
Jail
Landing Ground
City Museum Palace
Collectorate and S P Office
SBI
Sagar
Shiva Temple
Sarafa Bazar
New Tej Theatre
Clock Tower
Bajaja Bazar
Tipolia
Hope Circus
Jey Marg
Daudpur
Ashok Theatre
Alankar Hotel
Bus Stand
Mangal Marg
Alka Hotel
Hospital
Gopal Cinema
Company Bagh
Ashoka Hotel
Tourist Hotel
Tourist Information Bureau
GPO
Alwar Guest House
Dak Bungalow
Railway Station
To Industrial Area
Viney Marg
T B Hospital
To Delhi 170 km
Kothi Rao Guest House
Moti Doongri
Canal
R R College
Power House
Nehru Marg
Manu Marg
Stadium
Phool Bagh
Polytechnic
Polo Ground
Raghu Marg
Kheradeo
N
Canal
Circuit House
Samola
To Jaipur 148 km
Canal
Itarana
Bhugore
To Rajgarh 37 km
To Jaipur

which was once almost hunted to extinction by those who sought its meat and its beautiful spotted coat and by those who just wanted to shoot it for fun. Over 10,000 of the shy, nocturnal sambar, India's largest deer with a height of about 1.5 metres at the shoulder, roam the park and there are also numerous nilgai ('blue bull') and wild boar. Languar and rhesus monkeys, mongoose, jungle cat, civet, hyena, jackal, porcupine, caracel and ratel are amongst the other animals known to live in Sariska.

Sariska's birdlife is an interesting contrast to the species found in Bharatpur's Keoladeo Ghana sanctuary; here you find grey and black partridge, quail, red spurfowl, blossonheaded and rose ringed parakeets, sandgrouse, flycatcher, dove, woodpecker, shrike, peafowl, great horned owl, bee eater, nightjar and vulture.

. . . and when to see them

Sariska has three marked seasons—a relatively chilly winter when temperatures can fall below freezing during the nights in January, (there is a very brief spring), hot summers when 45°C is not uncommon in May and June and the monsoons when the heaviest rains fall between July and September. The best time to visit Sariska is between February and May/June: during the drier months the tigers, and also other animals, are drawn to the water pools and the park rangers have a better idea where to locate them. Avoid July and August.

Previously the Maharaja of Alwar and his guests went shooting here and they stayed in the splendid Sariska Palace which is now a hotel. Visitors to the park must be accompanied by an authorised guide.

The Alwar to Jaipur bus stops outside the gates to the Sariska Reserve.

Shekavati: Caravan Prosperity

Shekavati, covering desolate tracts of land on the eastern fringes of the Thar desert 130 km northeast of Jaipur, was a quasi-autonomous state within Dhundar. There were times in its history when it

Wall painting at Mandawa in the Shekavati region

enjoyed independence and its chiefs held power equal to that of the Kuchwaha rajas at Amber and Jaipur.

Islamicisation of Shekavati

Mokul, a 15th C ruler of these lands, prayed to Shekh Boorhan, an itinerant miracle-working Moslem saint, that he may be blessed with a son. In due course a boy was born and they called him Shekhji, in honour of the saint, and hence the region's name Shekavati. In further recognition of the saint Mokul dressed Shekhji with a buddea (strings worn crossways by Moslem children) and a blue robe and white cap—common attire amongst Moslems; he also abstained from eating pork and non-halal meat. Though the Shekawats were staunch Hindus—they fought courageously against Aurangzeb's destruction of their temples—aspects of Islam, dating from the time of Shekhji, became part of their tradition and culture. Today, at their capital of Jhunjhunu, there is one of Rajasthan's most important mosques.

Precious little grows in the wastes of Shekavati,

but once important caravan routes passed through these lands and the region prospered. As in Jaisalmer, wealthy merchant families evolved—they were known as Marwaris, derived from Marwar—and they traded in cloth, sugar, arms, dried fruits and herbs, gum arabic, spices, sandalwood and copper (copper is mined today at Khetri).

In the mid-19th C many Marwaris moved to Calcutta to involve themselves in the booming overseas trade. Business was lucrative and they sent money back home to their families who built splendid havelis (mansions) which they adorned with murals. The fashion in **wall paintings** reached its peak around the turn of this century. The interior and exterior of buildings were liberally and colourfully painted, and not only with the usual scenes from Hindu mythology and folklore, but also with depictions of contemporary things such as the bicycle, train, motorcar, aeroplane and events from the British Raj and famous figures, including Hitler. Sometimes old and new, east and west, come together and you may well see, for example, the Hindu monkey god Hanuman at the wheel of a car. As the Marwari merchants became more settled in their distant adopted cities they were joined by their families. Consequently the trend in haveli building and mural painting declined and came to an end by the 1940s. **Jhunjhunu** has old wall paintings dating from the 18th C but other places such as **Mandawa**, **Nawalgarh**, **Ramgarh**, **Bissau** and **Fatehpur** have more recent and more interesting havelis and murals.

Fantastic house murals

Today many a Shekavati village lies half deserted, its erstwhile occupants having left for the cities and large towns where there are jobs and business opportunities. The havelis are deteriorating and the murals are fading. Some of the old families do return to visit home, especially at the time of the Rani Sati festival, which is held at Jhunjhunu's Rani Sati temple to commemorate a girl who mounted her husband's funeral pyre in 1595.

Marwaris like Birla and Podor created some of

India's largest business empires. They donated funds to various charities and when you travel you will come across schools, hospitals, ashrams and temples which bear their names.

PRACTICAL INFORMATION

JAIPUR

As you would expect, Jaipur, Rajasthan's capital and main tourist centre, has a fair selection of hotels.

Amongst the best is the *Rambagh Palace*, Bhawani Singh Road (tel: 75141; telex: 036254 RBAG IN; managing group: Taj Hotels; 104 rooms, including suites; upper range price bracket), one of India's most famous and popular hotels. Initially an out-of-town residence for a favourite hand maiden, the Rambagh was converted into a hunting lodge in the mid 1800s; further additions were made to the complex and in the 1930s Maharaja Man Singh II turned the Rambagh into his official residence. In 1957 he set a precedent by being the first to open a palace as a hotel.

Set in lovely well kept gardens, the Rambagh has for the most part been tastefully converted into a luxury hotel, maintaining the old palace style and ambience while offering all modern facilities. Doormen and other staff are splendidly kitted out in traditional garb and they pamper their guests who recline like pukkah sahibs and memsahibs, wallowing in the romance and nostalgia of India's past. Stay in one of the old suites—and especially the lavish Maharaja's and Maharani's suites—and your dreams of the sumptious Orient will be complete.

Another of the Maharaja's residences was the *Raj Mahal* in Sardar Patel Road (tel: 69937; telex: 036313 JAI IN; managing group: Taj Hotels; upper range price bracket), which became the British Residency in 1921 and later home and guest house of Maharaja Man Singh II after he had vacated the Rambagh. Later it was opened as a small hotel, though little, it seemed, was changed and the walls of the palace still echoed the recent past when guests included the Queen and Prince Philip. Plans to revamp the Raj Mahal into a luxury hotel are underway and we will soon see how much of the old charm is sacrificed for the sake of modern comforts.

There are several large modern first class hotels in Jaipur. Most notable is the *Mansingh*, Sansar Chandra Road, off Agra Road (tel: 78771; telex: 036344 WLCO IN; managing group: Welcomgroup Hotels; 100 rooms; upper range price bracket). Others are: *Clark's Amer*, Jawahar Lal Nehru Marg (tel: 82216; upper range price bracket); *Jaipur Ashok*, Bani Park, Kantichandra Marg (tel: 75171; upper range price bracket); and *Jaipur Emerald, M I Marg (tel: 78681; upper range price bracket).*

Lesser palace hotels include the Rajasthan State Hotels Corporation's Khasa Kothi, off M I Marg and quite near the railway station (tel: 75151; mid-range price bracket), which is a spacious, colonial-style former royal guest house set in a large neat garden. The strutting, squawking peacocks add a further dash of local colour.

Various other royalty and Rajput nobles had their own palaces and mansions in Jaipur. In 1881 Narain Singh built the *Narain Niwas* which now stands near the road which bears his name. Today it is a 17-bedroomed hotel (tel: 65448; mid-range price bracket) decorated with its original late 19th C furnishings, including chandeliers, four-poster beds and British and local paintings.

Bissau Palace, Chandrapole Gate (tel: 74191; mid-range price bracket), was the Jaipur home of the ruler of the Bissau district (Shekavati). Family heirlooms decorate this small, homely and comfortable palace hotel.

Next door to the Bissau Palace is the even more modest *Khetri House Hotel* (tel: 69183; mid-range price bracket). At a pinch this small mansion can be called a palace hotel because it was the town residence of the rulers of Khetri, but really it is no more than a cosy 1930s Surrey-type middle class family home.

You can stay up in the Nahagarh fort at the *Durg restaurant*—there is only one room at present—from where there is a fabulous view over Jaipur; ask at the Tourist Office how you go about reserving the room.

Jaipur has three Tourist Bungalows: *Gangaur Tourist Bungalow*, M I Marg (tel:

60230), *Teej Tourist Bungalow*, Bani Park (tel: 74206)—both are in the mid-range price bracket—and the *Swagatam Tourist Bungalow*, near the railway station (tel: 67560; lower range price bracket). The Circuit House is off M I Marg, near Khasa Koti (tel: 74455).

Other more ordinary accommodation includes the clean, efficient, family-run *Arayan Niwas*, Sansar Chandra Road, behind the Amber Cinema (tel: 73456; mid-range price bracket); *Pink City*, M I Marg (tel: 72812; mid-range price bracket); *Achrol Lodge*, Civil Lines (tel: 72254; lower range price bracket); the *Golden Hotel*, Kanti Nagar (tel: 66606) and the *Jaipur Inn*, Bani Park (tel: 66057)—both are popular with backpackers and are in the lower range price bracket; the *Natraj*, M I Marg (tel: 61348); the *Prohit*, Vanasthali Marg (tel: 61974); and the *Radha Krishna* near the railway station (tel: 67352) are all in the lower range price bracket.

BHARATPUR

You come to Bharatpur for the birds and the most convenient places to stay are inside the grounds of the Keoladeo Ghana sanctuary. Top of the list is the *Bharatpur Forest Lodge* (tel: 2260; managing group: Ashok Hotels; upper range price bracket), a small, pleasant, modern hotel which is patronised by the better-off bird buffs. Nearby is the simple *Shanti Kutir Rest House* (tel: 2265; lower range price bracket).

The RTDC's *Saras Tourist Bungalow*, Fatehpur Sikri Road (tel: 2169; mid-range price bracket), is one of the better such establishments and is only a short walk from the sanctuary's entrance. Also within reasonable reach of the park is the *Govind Niwas Guest House*, Mathura Road (tel: 3347; mid-range price bracket), a large rambling family house now converted into a hotel; backpackers sometimes camp in the pretty gardens. Near the bus stand, in the centre of town, there are several inexpensive lodges: best known appears to be the *Tourist Lodge* (tel: 2850; lower range price bracket).

But best of all in Bharatpur is the *Gole Bagh* (tel: 3349; upper range price bracket), formerly the royal guest house which stands next to the old maharaja's palace. It recently underwent refurbishment and may only be open during the high season between October and February, but consult the Tourist Office for up-to-date information. The Gole Bagh is just out of town, away from the bustle of Bharatpur; the management offers excursions to the bird sanctuary.

Bharatpur's *Circuit House* is in Agra Road (tel: 2366).

DEEG, ALWAR AND SARISKA TIGER RESERVE

Deeg has no accommodation at present.

Alwar offers a cluster of modest hotels in the centre of town around Hope Circus, Manu Marg and the bus stand and there is a *Circuit House*, *DAK Bungalow* and *Railway Retiring Rooms*. Near the New Stadium, 2 km from the railway station, is the small family-run Phool Bagh Palace (tel: 2247). However, Alwar's most attractive hotel is the RTDC's 10-bedroomed *Lake Castle* (tel: 3764), a 19th C hunting lodge 13 km away overlooking Lake Siliserh.

37 km southwest of Alwar is the Sariska Tiger Reserve where you will find the splendid *Sariska Palace* (tel: 22; upper range price bracket), the grand, turn of the century hunting palace of the former maharaja of Alwar. At the edge of the reserve and surrounded by beautifully tranquil countryside, it is one of the more recent additions to the list of palace hotels and retains much of its former character. Room reservations can be made direct or in Delhi (tel: 732365) or Jaipur (tel: 66804).

At the entrance of the reserve is *Tiger Den* (tel: 42; mid- to upper range price bracket), one of the RTDC's best Tourist Bungalows and nearby is the simple *Forest Rest House* (lower range price bracket).

SAMOD

Samod, 41 km north of Jaipur, served as location for the TV series *Far Pavilions*. The palace in this delightful off-the-beaten-track village has been converted into a 15 bedroomed hotel. Reservations at the Samod Palace Hotel can be made at Samod House, Gangapole, Jaipur 302002 (tel: 4247; upper price range).

SHEKAVATI

Up until now Shekavati was a forgotten corner of Rajasthan little visited by outsiders—and hence there was no need for hotels. But now that the tourists are coming the demand for accommodation is on the increase, and one or two of the old merchant families and former nobility have converted their splendid havelis into hotels. Bear in mind when planning your trip that such places are few and far between.

The most interesting place to stay is the *Castle Mandawa* (tel: 23; mid- to upper price range bracket), a marvellous old fortified mansion which has been well decorated in local styles and has the basic mod cons—such as private bathrooms—but few of the less necessary luxuries. There are only 15 bedrooms/ suites (there are plans to expand), so in the high season it is wise to secure reservations. If you are coming from Jaipur these can be made at Old Mandawa House, Sansar Chandra Road, Jaipur 302001 (tel: 75358). Mandawa is 26 km southwest of Jhunjhunu, 168 km northwest of Jaipur and 211 km southwest of Delhi.

The 18th C fort at Dundlod (tel: 90), 150 km from Jaipur, offers rooms; they can be booked in Jaipur at Dundlod House, Hawa Sarak, Civil Lines (tel: 66276).

At the fascinating town of Nawalgarh, 32 km southwest of Jhunjhunu, you can stay at the *Roop Niwas Haveli* and in Jhunjhunu itself there is a pleasant, modern—though rather simple—hotel. There are some basic *DAK Bungalows* scattered around Shekavati and further accommodation is bound to open up in the future.

AJMER AND PUSHKAR

Internecine squabbles amongst their different clans was the root cause of the Rajputs' eventual downfall. Had they united on more occasions they would have been a formidable opposition to any invading army and maybe they could have prevented the early Moslems and even the Mughals from ever entrenching themselves in India. An old rift between the powerful Chauhan and Rathore clans left northwest India divided and allowed Mohammed Ghori the opportunity of a successful invasion. Defeated one by one, the Rajput clans scattered to re-establish themselves elsewhere, while Ghori's successors, now with Delhi in their hands, went on to found the Delhi Sultanate. The Moslems had won their foothold in India and from then on they became increasingly dominant.

Chauhans of Ajmer

The Chauhans were one of the great Rajput clans and prior to the Islamic invasion of India they 'claimed supremacy over all countries westward of the Indus, embracing the lands watered by its arms, from the foot of the Himalaya—the desert—to the Aravulli chain. The Chohan king... enumerated one hundred and eight great vassals, many of whom were subordinate princes' (Tod). Naturally their territories, which included Delhi, lay in the path of any armies pushing into India from the northwest.

In the 7th C AD the Chauhans founded Ajmer in a valley amidst the stark Aravalli hills and they gradually built it into a lovely garden city. Its strategic location amongst the hills of northeast Rajputana 395 km southwest of Delhi made it a valuable prize for any conquering force.

Rajput disunity and the Islamic onslaught

The Chauhans bitter rivalry with the Rathone clan who at that time ruled over the large neighbouring kingdom of Kanauj was to have profound repercussions in India. For when Mohammed

Ghori invaded India he took advantage of this Rajput disunity and attacked and defeated Prithviraj, the great Chauhan leader, at the Battle of Tarain in 1192 and then went onto rout Jaichand the Rathore. He captured Ajmer which served him as a foothold for further missions into Rajputana. It is believed that had the Rajputs combined their strength they could have withstood the Islamic onslaught.

Ajmer was fought over in following centuries and there were occasions when both the Sisodia and Rathore clans won the city back for the Rajputs, but in 1556 Akbar brought it into the fold of his Mughal empire and developed it as his military base and country residence.

The core of the Chauhans had long since scattered to the south to carve out new kingdoms for themselves with capitals at Bundi and Kotah.

Holy Ajmer

Founded in the 7th C by the Chauhan Rajputs, **Ajmer** was later dominated by the Mughals who realised the city's strategic significance as a base for controlling Rajputana. But Ajmer's Islamic heritage dates back to the 12th C and Muhammed Ghori and is most conspicuous today in the Dargah district of town.

Goal of Moslem pilgrimages

The fascinating tight network of alleys in the old **Moslem Dargah quarter** lead to the tomb of Mohinuddin Chisti (dargah means mausoleum), one of the holiest places of pilgrimage for Moslems in India. Mohinuddin Chisti was of Afghan descent, though he had been brought up in Persia, and was already an established holy man when he came to India with Muhammed Ghori's army at the end of the 12th C. He died in 1246 at the age of 97 and ever since his tomb has been venerated. Indeed, Akbar, a staunch devotee at his shrine, vowed he would walk from Agra to the Dargah, about 320 km, if his wife gave birth to a son. He fulfilled his promise—some say he did it barefoot—soon after the birth of Salim, later Emperor Jahangir.

Doing the washing at Ajmer

Visiting the holy site

A large whitewashed gate leads into the enclosed complex surrounding the Dargah. In the first courtyard there are two enormous cauldrons where you throw your donations—the offerings are later shared amongst those who look after the place. Above the inner gate, donated by the Nizam of Hyderabad in 1917, is the drum house and the two large drums are used to summon the faithful to prayer. Akbar and then Jahangir and Shah Jahan erected mosques and other buildings in the compound. In the centre of the Dargah you reach **Chisti's tomb** enclosed in a small white marble construction behind silver doors. Inside it is packed with pilgrims paying homage to Chisti and the walls are decorated with their precious donations. The air is close, scented by incense and the petals of fragrant flowers. 'Guides' pressure you to make contributions to the 'Dargah charity', and in the courtyard outside beggars and vendors of garlands and tithes beckon you to part with your money in return for some holy verses or an auspicious souvenir.

Every year the Urs Mela festival to mourn Chisti's death attracts over 100,000 pilgrims. Wealthy devotees pay to have the Dargah's cauldrons filled with kheer, a sweet porridge made of rice, milk, raisens and spices; the large pot holds 4480 kg while the smaller one has half the capacity.

According to an old custom 33 local families have the right to 'loot' the big cauldron, while another 27 families have a similar privilege over the small vessel. These families, traditionally poor and from the dhobi (washerman) caste, elect representatives who draw buckets of kheer (as the level goes down they climb down ladders into the steaming cauldron to reach the kheer) and hand them to their relatives to sell amongst the crowd of pilgrims. Hence the 'Looters of the Pot', as they are known, indirectly gain alms from the wealthy benefactors.

Emperor Humayun was once routed on the battlefield and pursued by his enemy to the edge of a river. He was forced to jump into the water

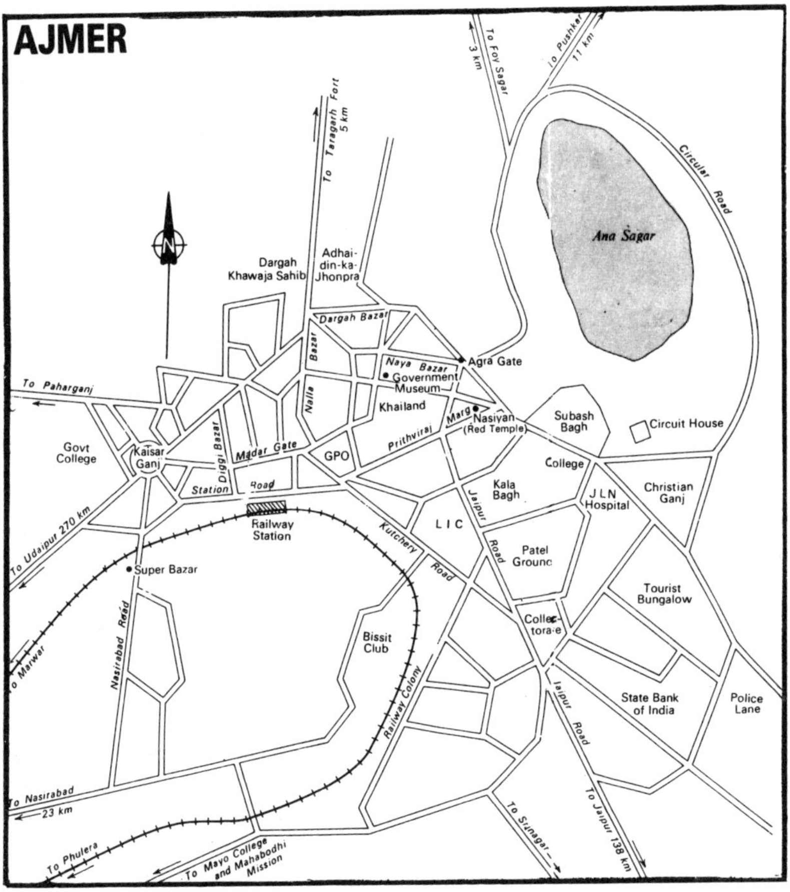

and was only saved from drowning by an old water carrier who dragged him onto the opposite shore. Apparently Humayun granted the man his wish to become king for the day and when he died soon after he buried him in the Dargah; his tomb is near to Chisti's.

A lane leads beyond the Dargah to an old place of worship called the **Adhai din ka Jhopra**, 'the two and a half day construction', so named because workers hurriedly built the mosque, completing it in two and a half days, so that Muhammed Ghori had somewhere to pray. Originally this was a

Sanskrit college and an impressive Brahma temple, and its pillars and other stones were used in the hasty construction of the mosque. Hence the Adhai din ka Jhopra has a mixture of Indo-Islamic design and is unique in its architecture. The facade is made up of seven arched screens, all profusely carved with Koranic inscriptions, and the impressive height of the long, narrow mosque was gained by stacking the old pillars on top of each other.

Perched on top of the desolate hill which rises behind Adhai din ka Jhopra are the remains of **Taragarh fort**, founded in 1100, commanding a view over both sides of the Aravallis. The fort itself may not warrant the tiring trek to the summit, but the panorama from here is spectacular.

Akbar's fort and residence in the centre of town, dating from 1570, is now a *museum* and includes archaeological finds from the surrounding countryside, 6th and 7th C Hindu sculptures, Rajput and Mughal armour and a collection of miniature paintings. Opening times are 10.00 to 17.00 (closed Fridays). Sir Thomas Roe, ambassador for the British, was received here by Emperor Jahangir.

Nearby is the bizarre 19th C red sandstone **Nasiyan and Soni Jain temple**, which must be one of the strangest and least expected of Rajasthan's sights: from a viewing gallery you look into a hall where wooden models depict scenes from Jain mythology. The stages of Rishabdevji's (Adinath's) life—his birth, his time as a prince at Ayodhya, his rejection of the world, his meditating under the banyon tree—are all represented as if they were a zany fantasy. Spectacular features include the palace, the coloured glass balls hanging from the ceiling and gods flying around in airships.

Zany fantasy

The artificial **Ana Sagar lake** was originally created in the 12th C by one of the Chauhan rulers to cleanse the battlefield made impure by the blood of his enemy. Emperors Jahangir and Shah Jahan later built marble pavilions on its banks and this is still a lovely spot in a city which today cannot boast the tranquil beauty it was once famed for.

The ghats at Pushkar

Another popular spot to pass the time or take a picnic is **Foy Sagar**—an artificial lake 5 km southwest of Ajmer—which was built in the 1890s as a reservoir for the city.

One of the many cultural legacies left by the British Raj in India was the public school and one of the most famous is **Mayo College**, founded in 1875 and named after Lord Mayo who was viceroy between 1869 and 1872, initially established to educate the sons of Rajputs. The school is just southeast of Ajmer's city centre.

Sacred Pushkar

Ajmer may be the destination for huge numbers of Moslem pilgrims each year, but neighbouring Pushkar is one of the most sacred places for Hindus in India. **Pushkar**, a delightful village amongst the hills and on the banks of a lake, lies an 11-km bus ride southeast of Ajmer on the other side of Nag Pahar, the Snake Mountain. The god Brahma rose up and slayed the demon Vijra Nabh with a lotus

Brahma slays the demon

leaf because he was killing his children. The petals of the flower fell in three places and from them arose three different lakes, one of which was Pushkar. The **Brahma temple** at Pushkar is the only temple in India dedicated to Brahma, the Creator. There are other temples, ashrams and ghats crowded along the waterfront and once there were even more of them before Aurangzeb, the fanatical Moslem emperor, plundered Pushkar, destroying many of its holiest shrines.

The time to come to Pushkar—whether you are a pious Hindu or an ordinary tourist—is during the full moon period of Kartik Poornima (October–November), when 100,000 or maybe even 200,000 pilgrims flock here in the belief that a dip in the lake at this time will absolve them of all their worldly sins and will ensure them a safe passage to heaven. With them they bring tens of thousands of cattle, camels and horses which they race, trade and put on show. It is a huge, lively, colourful, though rather dusty occasion, a mixture of intense spirituality and much fun in this serene and sacred setting. At night the men, topped with their exotic turbans, and the women, dressed in their gorgeous red cloths, cluster around small fires. There is a marvellous smell of smoke, spices, animals and dung in the crisp air. Itinerant actors, musicians and dancers enact well loved tales of chivalry and romance and, as a final gesture of faith, devotees set afloat tiny oil lamps on the lake in honour of Brahma.

Through the rest of the year a relative trickle of pilgrims pass through Pushkar. Nevertheless there is always a strong spiritual atmosphere here and whatever the season it is a pleasant and easygoing place to spend some time.

PRACTICAL INFORMATION

AJMER

Ajmer is a place travellers pass through while on their way to Pushkar (during the time of the festival) or when journeying from Jaipur to the southern parts of Rajasthan. Those who want to stop over in Ajmer will welcome the recent opening of the modern *Ajaymeru Hotel* (tel: 20089; managing group: Welcom group Hotels; upper range price bracket), which is down by the Ana Sagar Lake.

Previously the best place to stay had been the *Khadim Tourist Bungalow*. Savitri Girls' College Road (tel: 20490; mid-range price bracket), which is between the lake and the railway station. Or, if you can get permission to stay, there is a fine old colonial-style *Circuit House* (tel: 20795) on a hill in the Daulatbagh Gardens overlooking the lake.

There are several simple lower range price bracket hotels in the busy streets opposite the railway station, and these include the *Suriya*, the *Malwa* (tel: 23343) and the *Prithviraj* (tel: 23297).

PUSHKAR

Alternatively stay in nearby Pushkar where the pick of the accommodation is the marvellous *Sarovar Tourist Bungalow* (tel: 40), which was once one of the Maharaja of Jaipur's palaces. It only had a few rooms and due to demand a modern annexe has been constructed. Elsewhere in Pushkar there are many small and simple lodges catering for the backpacking traveller; some stay a while and rent their own place.

The Pushkar mela (mela means festival and a lakhi mela, such as the Pushkar mela and the Urs mela, is a festival with at least 100,000 in attendance) also attracts thousands of tourists. To accommodate them the RTDC erects *Tent City* comprising hundreds of tents of deluxe, ordinary and dormitory standards; prices range from the lower to upper bracket. Beds and bed clothes and three meals a day are provided in the deluxe and ordinary tariffs; there are portable Western-style washing and toilet facilities.

Tent City tends to get heavily booked up in advance. For reservations and further information contact:

The General Manager
RTDC
Usha Niwas
Kalyan Path
Jaipur 302004
Tel: 79252

The Assistant Director
Rajasthan Tourism
Chandralok
36 Janpath
New Delhi 110001
Tel: 322332

THE BUNDI AND KOTAH REGION

The Harachauhans, descendants of the once illustrious Chauhan line, established their homeland in southeast Rajputana after the defeat of Prithviraj by Muhammed Ghori. They formed close ties with the neighbouring Sisodia clan and often fought alongside them against the Moslems. They did, though, eventually sign a treaty with Akbar. The respect of a person's dignity was paramount in these protocols—to pamper status, albeit with rather cosmetic privileges, did much to sooth relationships—and in these terms the Harachauhans were given a fairly honourable deal by Akbar.

The Harachauhans of Haravati

A group of Chauhans who survived Muhammed Ghori's sword at the Battle of Tarain in 1192 fled south and carved a small principality for themselves in southeast Rajputana. Known as the Harachauhans or simply the Haras, under the leadership of Rao Devi Singh they defeated the Meena tribes of Bandu ka Nal in 1342. The Haras renamed this remote corner Haravati and founded their city of Bundi some 135 km northeast of the Mewar capital of Chittorgarh. They established kinship and military ties with the Sisodias and for a while they were quasi-vassals of Mewar.

Over the following centuries the Haras struggled to maintain their boundaries, but once Akbar was on the throne they were no match against the Mughal might which swept through Rajputana, and in 1569 Rao Surjan II of Bundi conceded Ranthambor, a crucial Rajput fort, to the emperor.

Akbar allowed the rulers of Bundi certain unique privileges:

'1st. That the chiefs of Boondi should be exempted from that custom, degrading to a rajpoot, of sending a dola (Dola is a term for a princess affianced to the King).

'2nd. Exemption from the jezeya, or poll tax.

The main gate into Bundi's fort

'3rd. The chiefs of Boondi should not be compelled to cross the Attoc.

'4th. That the vassals of Boondi should be exempted from the obligation of sending their wives or female relatives "to hold a stall in the Meena Bazaar" at the palace, on the festival of Noroza.

'5th. That they should have the privilege of entering the Dewan-aum, or "hall of audience", completely armed.

'6th. That their sacred edifices should be respected.

'7th. That they should never be placed under the command of a Hindu leader.

'8th. That their horses should not be branded with the imperial dagh.

'9th. That they should be allowed to beat their nakarras, or "kettle-drums" in the streets of the capital, as far as the lal durwaza, or "red gate"; and that they should not be commanded to make the "prostration", on entering the Presence.

'10th. That Boondi should be to the Haras what Delhi was to the king, who should guarantee them from any change of capital' (Tod).

Honourable peace

Whether the rulers of Bundi did really enjoy all these privileges is questionable, but without doubt they did achieve a more honourable relationship—in Rajput terms—with the Mughals than any other Rajput clan, with the exception of the Sisodias who continued to fight for their independence.

The Haras benefited from their bond with the Mughals. In 1631 Emperor Jahangir granted Madho Singh the district of Kotah for services to the empire and under Shah Jahan the Hara Chattar Sal was governor of Delhi. During this period of stability the Haras were able to initiate an impressive building programme and at the same time their arts flourished.

Bundi of Uneasy Dreams

Bundi remains relatively remote and off the beaten track—it has no railway nor any hotels (there is talk, though, of building accommodation for tourists). Nevertheless, it is a fascinating old town overlooked by one of the finest palace forts in Rajasthan.

'The coup d'oeil of the castellated palace of Boondi, from which ever side you approach it, is perhaps the most striking in India' (Tod). And more recently Rudyard Kipling was equally impressed by what he saw at Bundi: 'Jeypore Palace may be called the Versailles of India; Udaipur's House of State is dwarfed by the hills round it and the spread of the Pichola Lake; Jodhpur's House of strife, grey towers on red rock, is the work of giants; but the Palace of Bundi, even in broad daylight, is such a palace as men build for themselves in uneasy dreams—the work of goblins rather than of men'.

Goblin palace

The spectacular **palace** rises from the slopes of a hill. Below is the town, and the former pleasure gardens and ghats lead down to the rectangular Naval Sagar tank (in the middle is a temple dedicated to Varuna, god of water) which served as the main source of water. The immense and impregnable walls enclose a huge area including the palace complex, the old city and Taragarh, the fortified refuge which was built up on the summit of the hill in 1372.

The palace stands deserted and little cared for. It is a steep walk up the cobbled path to the characteristically imposing *main gate*, where the statues of two elephants form an arch over the main entrance. Just inside the porch you can still see the old *water clock*; a container was floated on water and drops were allowed to fall into it. Exactly every half hour it would sink, informing the timekeeper that it was time to hit the gong and announce the end of a period to the rest of the palace.

Though the fort was founded in the 14th C its grander embellishments date from the 16th and 17th C and they show a marked fusion between Mughal and traditional Rajput decoration and architecture. The watchman will show you around the many empty chambers. Above and on the opposite side of the first courtyard is the *royal bal-*

cony where the rao sat in audience on the white marble throne. Make sure you see the *cloisters* running round the Chittra Sala quadrangle where miniature murals in blues and greens depict the mythological tale of Krishna and Radha. In another section of the palace hang the dusty portraits of former rulers. The views from the palace over the city and the plains beyond are splendid. Opening times are 09.00 to 16.30.

There are lovely wooded gardens along the banks of the large **Jait Sagar tank** just to the north of Bundi and they are within an easy bike ride of town. The small **Sukh Mahal**, once a royal summer lodge, has a pretty setting overlooking the lake and is now used as a rest house for visiting officials and, sometimes, tourists (enquire at the Tourist Office). Continuing along the lakeside path you pass the **Kshar Barg** where a cluster of cenotaphs of past raos stand neglected in an overgrown enclosed garden. **Shikar Burj**, a little beyond, was built by Rao Ummed Singh as a hunting lodge in 1770 and today it is a popular picnic spot with locals. Further on, some 8 km northwest of Bundi, you reach **Phool Mahal** (Flower Palace) and **Phool Sagar** (Flower Lake), which is the present home of the erstwhile royal family of Bundi. The palace was built earlier this century (hence it is sometimes called New Palace) and its formal gardens, the large banquet hall and some of the other notable rooms can only be visited with special permission from the palace (tel: 1, or arrangements can be made through the Tourist Office).

Along the lakeside

Back amongst the bustle in the centre of town and not far from the old city's Chogan Gate is the **Raniji ki Baori**, an ornate and elaborately carved archway with a wide flight of steps leading down to a 42-metre-deep well; it was commissioned by one of the Bundi princesses to provide water for thirsty travellers and citizens. On the southern edge of town, next to the Kotah road, is the locally famous 17th C 84-pillared **cenotaph**.

Southwest of Bundi, 48 km on the road to Chittor, are the 12th C remains of the once great complex of **Shiva temples at Menal**, which flourished at the time of the Chauhan Prithviraj. 16 km further on are the crumbled ruins of **Bijolia**, another important 12th C temple complex, which today has only three of its 100 temples still standing.

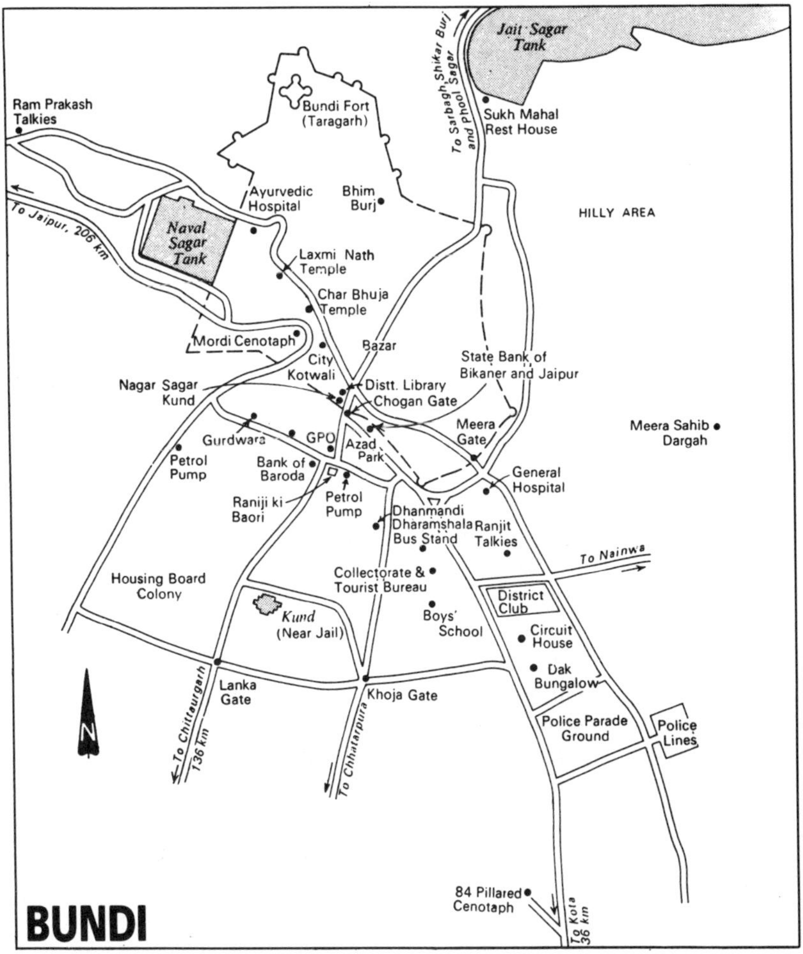

Fortress and Fission at Kotah

Kotah was the capital of a splinter group of Hara-chauhans who had established their own state, independent from their fellow clansmen at Bundi, on the banks of the river Chambal. Today Kotah, with a population of over 300,000, is one of Rajasthan's main commercial centres with Asia's largest fertiliser plant and an important nuclear research station amongst its modern industries.

Like Bundi, only 36 km to the northwest, Kotah has not really been discovered by tourists, partly because this corner of Rajasthan is off the main tourist circuit and also because Kotah is not one of the spectacular cities of Rajasthan. Nevertheless, amongst the modern buzz there is—as in any advanced city in India—the equally frenetic traditional way of life. And Kotah does offer you a palace fort which is worth a visit, not so much for imposing and grand architecture, rather for the excellent museums it contains.

Excellent museums

The **fort**, enclosed by the old city walls in the centre of the present town, is built on fairly flat land overlooking the River Chambal. Entrance is through a gateway flanked by two large carved elephants. Inside, the *Rao Madho Singh Museum* has an exquisite collection of Rajput miniature paintings from the celebrated Kotah school as well as costumes, weapons, sculptures, frescoes and other art. Opening times are 11.00 to 17.00; closed Friday. In the *Government Museum* you will find rare coins and manuscripts and more sculptures. Opening times are 10.00 to 17.00; closed Fridays.

On the River Chambal, opposite the fort, is the **Kotah Barrage**, a major irrigation project constructed to divert the river's waters into canals. Upstream and on the same side as the fort are the **Chambal Gardens** where locals come and stroll in the evening. There is nothing special about the gardens—though curiously there is one pond stocked with both crocodiles and flamingoes. You can take a boat to **Jag Mandir**, the holy monument in the middle of Kishor Sagar, the large tank in

Crocodiles and flamingoes

the centre of town. On the banks of the tank, near the Tourist Office, are a group of dilapitated cenotaphs.

11 km east of Kotah is the old **Tod's bridge**, built by Lieutenant Colonel James Tod when he was serving as a British political agent in Rajputana.

Temple Sites Around Kotah

There are numerous ancient and tumble-down temple complexes scattered around Rajasthan and one

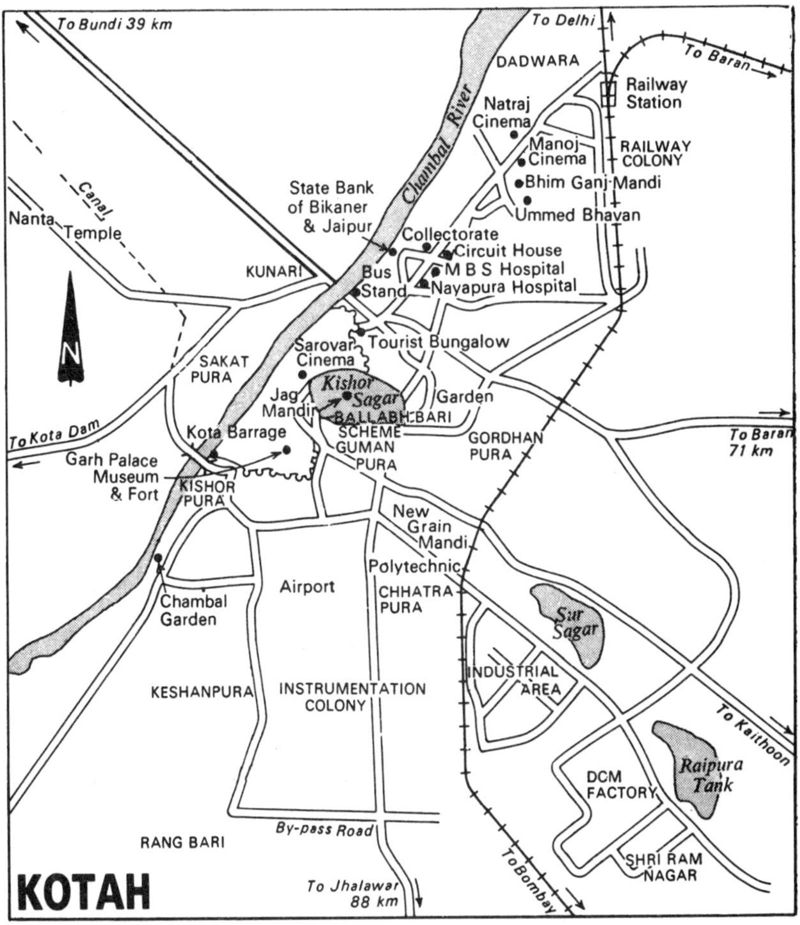

of the finest sites in this region is at **Baroli**, 40 km southwest of Kotah, which dates back to the 9th C. Aurangzeb, who was so fanatically anti-Hindu, ordered the vandalisation of many Hindu shrines and the temples at Baroli were amongst those to suffer. The **Ghatesvara Shiva temple** still stands, though its carved nymphettes have been badly damaged. Some of the sculptures and crafted stonework is now housed at the Government Museum in Kotah. Beyond is the large **Rana Pratap Sagar,** a dammed lake and an important water supply named after the 16th C Sisodia hero.

Jhalarapatan, near Jhalawar, some 60 km southeast of Kotah, is another once magnificent temple site. This was the 8th–9th C City of Bells where Hindu temples stood—the elaborately-carved **Sun temple** is still spectacular—and nearby there are Jain temples and the relics of Buddhist cave temples. Pieces retrieved from the complex can be seen at the Jhalawar museum.

And there are more famous temples at **Ramgarh**, 64 km to the east of Kotah (the last part is accessible by jeep), though they are not so ancient. The most important is the **Bhandadevara Shiva temple**; older 10th C Jain caves are in the forests 5 km away.

Wildlife Sanctuaries

Three wildlife sanctuaries are in the catchment area of Kotah. The length of the River Chambal from Rana Pratap Sagar to its confluence with the Yamuna is the **Gavial National Sanctuary** and in the winter months you can take a boat out and see gavials (long-snouted crocodiles, known locally as gharials) nesting on the banks. **Bhensrod Garh Sanctuary,** 53 km from Kotah, around Rawatbhutah in Chittor district, is a reserve for leopards and other more common game. 60 km southeast of Kotah is the **Darrah Sanctuary** where game includes a few tigers, panther, sloth bear, wild boar, nilgai and various deer.

The most important game park is **Sawai Madhopur**, 110 km northeast of Kotah and on the main

Ranthambore citadel—ghosts of mass suicides

Bombay-Kotah-Delhi railway line. It is one of Rajasthan's two tiger reserves, the other being Sariska. Theforests of Sawai Madhopur became a favourite hunting ground of the royal household of Jaipur and their old lodges have now been converted into accommodation. The park, now a sanctuary under Project Tiger, covers about 400 sq km of dhak forests and more open woodlands, and game includes around 40 tigers, plus leopard, panther, jackal, sambhar, chital, nilgai, wildboar, chinkara, langaur, hyena, sloth bear and crocodiles basking on the shores of the lakes. Amongst the birds at Sawai Madhopur are partridge, paradise flycatcher, red spurfowl, pea fowl, green pigeon, quail, lapwing, sand grouse, king and whitebacked vultures, crested serpent eagle, black stork, teal, pintail, grey lag goose and, at night, the night jar and spotted owl. Entrance is permitted only with a local guide and the best season to come is between November and May—in March the dhak, 'red flame of the forest', bursts into colour.

On the edge of the park are the ancient and ghostly ruins of **Ranthambore**, an extensive and once powerful citadel which was passionately fought over in the past and is now slowly deteriorating under nature.

Founded in the mid-10th C by the Chauhans, the fort defended the eastern limits of Rajputana from its hilltop vantage. In 1298 Alaudin laid siege to Ranthambore and he eventually won his prize after Hammira, one of the legendary Rajput heroes, ordered his women to perform the ritual johar while he and his men battled to their inevitable death.

Mass suicide

Over the following centuries Ranthambore passed between the Rajput and Moslem strongmen of the day. In the mid-15th C Rana Kumbha of Mewar recaptured it for the Rajputs. Later it passed into the hands of the Haras of Bundi who lost it to Akbar in 1569. After the death of Aurangzeb the rulers of Jaipur took possession before finally abandoning it.

A few monuments from the past still stand, not too decrepit to evoke something of their history. But more important is the fort's 8th C *Ganesh shrine* which attracts many more pilgrims than the castle does visitors—especially at the time of Bhadrapad Sudi Chaturthi when there is a special festival.

PRACTICAL INFORMATION

BUNDI

Maybe a hotel or two will be built in Bundi now that tourists have discovered this delightful, out-of-the-way palace city. But up to now the accommodation has been limited to a rather shabby *Circuit House* (tel: 6) near the bus station and a *DAK Bungalow*.

KOTAH

The bulk of the people passing through Kotah are mid-ranking businessmen and officials and most of the accommodation —rather ordinary, modern-style hotels —cater for them. But there is one special place, the 1930s *Brij Raj Bhavan Palace* (tel: 3071; managing group: Indotel; upper range price bracket), which you will find in a quiet spot overlooking the Chambal River. It has only a few rooms and they are still decorated with their original furnishings and family heirlooms—including pictures of Queen Mary of England who stayed here in 1911—and, though the Brij Raj Bhavan is not one of the fanciest palace hotels, it is certainly one of the most charming.

The other hotels include: the *Chambal Tourist Bungalow*, near Kishor Sagar (tel: 6527; mid-range price bracket); the *Circuit House* (tel: 3620); the *Navrang*, Civil Lines (tel: 3294); the *Payal*, Nayapura (tel: 5401); and the *Jagdish*, near the bus station (tel: 3414)—all are in the mid- to lower range price brackets.

SAWAI MADHOPUR

Sawai Madhopur has a couple of cheap lodges near the station, but you will find more interesting accommodation on the road to the tiger sanctuary.

First you come to the *Maharaja's Lodge* (Mid-range price bracket), once the guest house for the Maharaja of Jaipur's shooting friends. It was built earlier this century and lies amidst pleasant gardens; now, however, the lodge is in need of refurbishment—or at least a lick of paint to cleanse it of its mustiness (the job perhaps done by the time you arrive).

Continue, and about 5 km from Sawai Madhopur you come to the maharaja's own residence, *Castle Jhoomar Bhaori* (tel: 620; mid-range price bracket), which is now one of the best and most unusual of the RTDC's 'Tourist Bungalows'. Isolated and perched on one of the wooded hills above the road, it looks—with its strange architecture and candy green coat of paint—like a small fairy tale palace. There is nothing grand about the place, though it has character and has been attractively furnished and decorated in traditional styles. Outings to Ranthambore and around the sanctuary can be arranged from here.

Tucked away and overlooking a lake near the entrance of the sanctuary you will find the *Jogi Mahal*, an old 'watch-out' pavilion and an ideal vantage for spotting game. Inside it has been simply but tastefully renovated and accommodation comprises two bedrooms and bathroom. Who can give you permission to stay here seems to be a moot point; however it is run by the Forest Commission, so consult them in Delhi, Jaipur or Sawai Madhopur (the Field Director's office is near the railway station). Bring your own provisions.

Public transport between Sawai Madhopur and the sanctuary at Ranthambore is scarce; by the station you will find horse-drawn buggies and maybe a taxi; alternatively try to hitch a lift.

THE UDAIPUR AND CHITTORGARH REGION

In an age of honour the Sisodias were the most hallowed of the Rajput clans. They were admired for their stoicism and uncompromising stand against the more powerful Moslem armies. Self-imposed death was the ultimate sacrifice and the Sisodias were the most ready to perform the necessary ritual: on three famous occasions when faced with defeat they committed the ghastly johar. Decimated in numbers and so often at battle with the Moslems, the Sisodias suffered in terms of wealth, but their prestige was always highest amongst the clans and their heroes, such as Padmini, Rana Sanga, Rana Kumbha and Rana Pratap, are some of the most revered in Rajput legend.

The Sisodias of Mewar

Of the Rajput clans the Sisodias of the old Mewar principality were the most respected:

'The Hindu tribes yield unanimous suffrage to the prince of Mewar as the legitimate heir to the throne of Rama, and style him Hindu Sooraj, or "Sun of the Hindus". He is universally allowed to be the first of the "thirty-six royal tribes"; nor has a doubt ever been raised respecting his purity of descent' (Tod).

True to their honoured position, the Sisodias were the most proud and gallant of the Rajputs, prefering to fight the Mughals in order to retain their integrity and independence, rather than choose the more comfortable option of coming to terms with the Mughals through matrimony or treaty as other Rajput royal families had done.

Chittorgarh, the oldest fort in Rajasthan

The Sisodias—sometimes known as the Guhilotes, after Guhil, a 6th C ancestor—had long been established in the region of Mewar and their citadel capital at Chittor is believed to be the oldest fort in Rajasthan. Thrice the citizens of Chittorgarh suffered the full horrors of siege because they refused to submit to their enemies, and the celebrated tale about Padmini, a famed 13th C Sisodia beauty, amply illustrates the courageous and dogmatic character of these Rajputs.

The romantics insist that Alaudin, the powerful sultan of Delhi, laid siege to Chittorgarh in 1303 so he could get hold of Padmini; the more prosaic explanation is that his objective was territorial gain rather than a jewel for his harem. Whatever his reasons, the story continues that the siege ended in stalemate and in the compromise it was agreed that Alaudin could have a look at Padmini—in contravention of the Rajputs' strict code of purdah. The sultan was ushered into a chamber where, through a mirror, he caught a glimpse of Padmini descending the steps to her pool. Infatuated, he turned to get a better look, but his path to the window was barred. Foolishly Bhim Singh, Padmini's husband, escorted Alaudin out of the fort, where he was ambushed and taken hostage. Naturally, Padmini was the ransom. She sent a message, agreeing to barter herself for her husband's life and immediately set about arranging a grand entourage to take her to the sultan. But inside each of the 700 palaquins she hid armed soldiers in place of handmaidens and on arriving at Alaudin's camp the disguise was thrown off, a battle ensued and Bhim Singh escaped.

The beauty and the sultan

In retaliation Alaudin stepped up his pressure against Chittorgarh, until the Sisodias had little option than to submit or fight to the death. Orders were given to prepare for the johar; meanwhile the men, donned in their symbolic saffron robes, solemnly readied themselves for their final battle. They fought to the end while the thousands of wives and sisters, chanting verses from the holy Gita, filed into the furnace-like subterranean chamber where they burnt to death. Padmini supervised the awful event and then, after the last of the women had been engulfed by flames, she herself stepped into the inferno.

A hundred or so years later, in the mid-1400s,

the Sisodias experienced one of their greatest epochs under the leadership of Rana Kumbha. A fine soldier who once captured Ajmer from the Moslems, Rana Kumbha is best remembered though as a prolific builder, and 32 Rajputana forts—including Mandalgarh, Achalgarh, Macheen, Ahore and the formidble Kumbhalgarh—are credited to him.

In the early 16th C Mewar reached the summit of her prosperity under Rana Sanga, but these glorious days were dramatically cut short with the arrival of the Mughals. In 1519 Barbur crossed the River Indus, eight years later he defeated the united Rajput forces led by Rana Sangam at the Battle of Kanauj and went on to establish the Mughal dynasty at Delhi. Even today local folklore recounts Rana Sanga's prowess on the battlefield and boasts his scars of war—which included the loss of an eye and a hand and 84 wounds to the body—as if they were medals won in action.

Soon after, in 1535, Chittorgarh suffered its second sacking, this time at the hands of Bahadur Shah, the Sultan of Gujarat, when 13,000 women are said to have burnt in the johar. In the subsequent confusion Banbir claimed right to the Sisodias' gaadi, though Udai Singh was the legitimate heir.

Udai Singh was only a baby, nevertheless he posed a potential threat to Banbir. Panna, Udai's nurse, realised her ward was in danger and had the baby smuggled out of Chittorgarh, placing her own child in the royal cot as a substitute. Banbir killed Panna's baby, thinking he was Udai Singh, and thus believed his position was secure from opposition. But when Udai Singh grew up he deposed Banbir to win his rightful inheritance. As it turned out, he lacked courage and 'had not quality of a sovereign; and wanting martial virtue, the common heritage of his race, he was destitute of all' (Tod). When Chittorgarh was attacked for the third time in 1568 by Akbar, Udai Singh fled.

Udai Singh's weakness proved to be a blessing in disguise. He chose to abandon the ill-fated

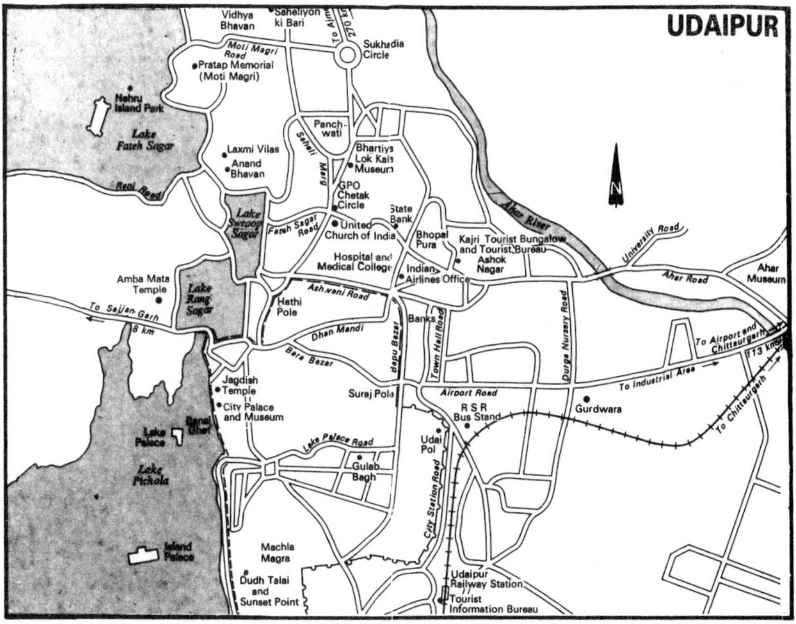

Founding of Udaipur

citadel of Chittorgarh and created a new capital in a valley 112 km to the west. Udaipur, named after its founder, was as much in contrast with the typical fortified strongholds of Rajputana as Udai Singh was with the characteristic fiery Rajput heroes. Udai Singh's city, with its graceful palaces reflected in the lake's glasslike waters, is one of the loveliest in India.

While Udai Singh was rather an oddball Rajput, his son and heir, Rana Pratap, personalified best the famed Rajput qualities of chivalry, patriotism and honour. Rana Pratap succeeded his father in 1572 at a time when Akbar was extending his influence in Rajputana by courting friendship with the Rajput rulers and sometimes cementing these bonds with matrimony; failing that Akbar would attempt to get what he wanted through agression. Rana Pratap obstinately refused to be drawn into an alliance with the Mughals and this led to a face to face encounter with Man Singh, the Kuchwaha

Rajput who was, nevertheless, one of Akbar's finest generals.

The conflict between Rana Pratap's Rajput army and Man Singh's Mughal force is the most celebrated battle in the annals of Rajputana. It took place on 3 April 1576 around the Haldigathi Pass, 43 km north of Udaipur. The Sisodias' smaller, less well equipped army initially held the upper hand; indeed a spear thrown by Rana Pratap lodged in the side of Man Singh's howdah and only narrowly missed killing him. But the tide changed; Pratap was chased off the battlefield and it was only thanks to the speed and stamina of his horse Chetak that he was able to reach safety. Chetak collapsed from exhaustion and wounds and the spot where he died is marked by a cenotaph. Today the daily express train between Delhi and Udaipur is named in honour of the legendary horse.

Most celebrated battle

Rana Pratap, with his family and a small band of survivors, retreated to the hills where he lived under cover for several years, often protected by the local Bhil tribesmen. He gradually gathered more followers and by the time of his death in 1597 he had recaptured much of Mewar from the Mughals; ironically, though, Chittorgarh, that great symbol of Rajput heroism, eluded him.

Lakeside Splendour

Udai Singh founded **Udaipur** in 1568 in a lovely valley virtually surrounded by hills, and he transferred the capital of Mewar here from the ancient and historic fortress city of Chittor, 112 km to the east. Later rulers continued his work in their own gracious styles. Today there is no spot in any Indian city which can compare in beauty with Lake Pichola and its romantic palaces and colourful ghats.

The splendid **City Palace** stretches 250 metres along the eastern shores of Lake Pichola. At its core is the original stronghold initiated by Udai Singh in the 1530s. It is quite surprising that the many additions to the palace, built over the following

Jag Nivas Lake Palace, now a hotel

generations in various styles, work together so harmoniously. The main entrance on the north side is through *Bari Pol* and then *Tripolia*. Between these two gates are eight arches where past rulers were weighed against gold and silver which was then handed out to the poor. Beyond Tripolia is where the elephant fights used to take place.

Palaces within the palace

Inside the palace a maze of corridors lead to smaller exquisite palaces, chambers, courtyards and gardens, each with its individual character. In *Mor Chowk*, Peacock Yard, mosaic peacocks made from coloured stones, glass and semi-precious gems are set in niches and represent the three seasons—summer, winter and the rains.

The *Krishna Vilas*, its walls covered with miniature paintings of festivals and other colourful and happy occasions, is dedicated to a tragic 16-year-old girl, Krishna Kumari, daughter of a 19th C maharana. Princes from the rival Jaipur and Jodhpur households both wanted to marry her and this left her father in a quandry as who to pick because he feared to antagonise either party—both Jaipur and Jodhpur were, at this stage, more powerful than Udaipur. Krishna Kumari solved the dilemma by killing herself with an overdose of opium. Her father decorated this room in her honour.

The early 18th C *Chini Chritrashala*, the Chinese Gallery, is partly covered with blue and white Chinese tiles; there are also Dutch tiles depicting scenes from the bible. Other rooms or apartments include the *Dilkhush Mahal*, which is notable for its frescoes; the *Baari Mahal*, with its lovely courtyard—both date from the 17th C; *Moti Mahal* and *Shish Mahal*, worth a visit for their stained glass and mirror work. You can see murals portraying Radha Krishna stories in the *Bhim Mahal* and the Manak Mahal has a collection of porcelain figures. There is still more to see in the *Zenana Mahal*, the Queens' Palace.

The *armoury* includes armour worn by Rana Pratap and large murals in the outer courtyards show the Sisodia hero gallantly fighting to preserve Rajput honour. There is a wonderful display of more realistic portraits, and also photos, of other maharanas and influential Britons of India's past. Gathering dust in one of the yards is an early 20th C Rolls Royce.

Opening times of the City Palace are 09.30 to 16.30.

Much of the City Palace's charm is its marvellous setting overlooking **Lake Pichola**. You can wake up to these views by staying in a royal suite at the **Shiv Niwas**, the southern section of the City Palace which has now been converted into one of India's most fabulous palace hotels. Another part of the palace is still occupied by the descendants of the erstwhile royal family.

Lake palace hotels

Unique, though, is the **Jag Nivas Lake Palace** rising straight out of the calm waters in the middle of Lake Pichola. Standing on 1.6 hectares of submerged rock, the white marble and granite palace was built in the 17th C by Maharana Jagat Singh as a summer residence and was converted by Bhagwat

The Garden of the Maids of Honour—Seheliyon ki Bari—at Udaipur

Singh, one of his descendants, into a hotel in 1963.

Amer Singh started the construction of **Jag Mandir**, the other man-made island in Lake Pichola; it was completed seven years later, in 1615, by Karen Singh. Jagat Singh made his own additions and hence the name Jag Mandir. There is a three-storey tower on the island and a small mosque dedicated to a Moslem saint. The Sisodia ruler of the day allowed Prince Khurrum (later Emperor Shah Jahan) to take refuge on Jag Mandir after his aborted coup against his father Emperor Jahangir. There are plans to build a hotel on the island, though at the moment the only inhabitants are hundreds of parakeets. It is possible to take a boat to either of the lake islands from the jetty below the City Palace, and the views are particularly beautiful when the sun casts its final golden rays on the walls of the City Palace and the ghats.

Pleasant pastimes

The **ghats**, which lead down to the water's edge on the eastern shores of Lake Pichola, are a fascinating place to while away some hours. It is a lively and colourful scene when the locals come to pray and wash here in the early morning and evening cool. Pleasant, though not such a priority, is a wander in the **Sajjan Niwas Gardens**—and the neighbouring **Gulab Bagh**, or Rose Garden—on the other side (south side) of the City Palace. The 40 hectare gardens bordering Lake Pichola were created by Maharana Sajjan Singh in the late 19th C, and attractions include a small zoo and a children's railway.

Lake Fateh Sagar, Udaipur's other main lake, is just to the north of Lake Pichola and was originally constructed by Maharana Jai Singh in 1678. But heavy rains destroyed the dam which contained the waters and so, in 1754, Maharana Fateh Singh rebuilt the lake and named it after himself. **Nehru Park**, a 1.8-hectare island in the middle of Lake Fateh Sagar, is a neat formal garden with pavilions, fountains—the sprays are coloured by red, blue and green spotlights—and a boat-shaped café. Many couples and families stroll their evenings away at Nehru Park; you can catch a motor launch or hire a paddle raft from the foot of Moti Magri.

Having surveyed the surrounding valleys from the summit of **Moti Magri**—the hill overlooking the present Lake Fateh Sagar from the eastern shores—Udai Singh chose the lands below for the site of his new city. Terraced gardens, including a Japanese rockery, now cover the slopes of Moti Magri. At the top there is an imposing statue—not of Udai Singh as you might have supposed, but of Rana Pratap, Rajasthan's favourite hero astride his faithful Chetak. Moti Magri, Pearl Hill, is open from 09.00 to 18.00.

Away from the Lakes

Away from the lakeshores, but only 150 metres north of the City Palace, is the **Jagdish Temple**, Udaipur's most impressive shrine. Built in 1651 by—once again—Jagat Singh, the elaborately carved temple at the top of a long flight of steps has a black stone effigy of Vishnu as its main object of veneration.

While all the bustle within the narrow lanes of the old city walls can claim to be part of the traditional character, the urban chaos in the modern city outside cannot claim such quaint pretence. But modern Udaipur does have quiet, spacious and leafy residential districts. The **Saheliyon ki Bari**, the Garden of the Maids of Honour, is a lovely ornamental courtyard with a pool and kiosks which spout water in all directions from their domes; it was built by Maharana Sangam Singh for the maids of the royal household. Opening times are 09.00 to 18.00; for a nominal charge you can have the fountains turned on.

Modern Udaipur

Walk down Saheliyon ki Bari road, towards the town centre, and you will come to **Bhartiya Lok Kala Mandal**, a delightful *folklore museum*. It was established in 1952 and its collection includes traditional costumes, masks, musical instruments, paintings, all sorts of models and puppets. Besides being a museum, Lok Kala Mandal is an internationally acclaimed *school of puppetery*. Puppet shows are performed here daily. Opening times are 09.00 to 18.00.

East of Udaipur, 3 km, are the ruins of **Ahar**, an ancient capital of Mewar. More recent royalty were buried here and the most conspicuous cenotaphs commemorate Maharanas Amar Singh (1621) and Sangam Singh (1734). Ahar's small archaeological museum is open from 09.30 to 16.30.

In the other direction, 5 km west of Udaipur, Sajjan Singh built a hunting lodge, **Sajjan Garh**, on top of a steep hill. The panoramic views from here are fantastic and on a clear day they say you can see Chittorgarh 112 km to the northeast. Enquire at the Tourist Office about permission to visit Sajjan Garh.

Excursions North of Udaipur

There are many places worth visiting around Udaipur and most can be reached by public transport.

There is a daily RTDC excursion to Eklingji, Nagda, Haldighati and Nathdwara; the tour bus leaves from outside Udaipur's Tourist Bungalow in the afternoon.

The **Eklingji temple** in the village of **Kailashpur** 22 km north of Udaipur is dedicated to the tutelary god of the royal Sisodia family. Here in the 8th C Bappa Rawal, founder of the Sisodia dynasty, received a prophecy from a sadhu who forecast a glorious future for his lineage. A Shiva lingam in the oldest part of the temple (AD 734) marks the spot where this encounter took place and there is a statue of Bappa Rawal in the courtyard. The central temple is made of white marble and, beyond its silver screens, it enshrines a four-faced image of Shiva carved out of black marble. There is a bronze statue of a bull which is particularly auspicious: Alaudin, while on his mission to suppress Mewar at the end of the 13th C, attempted to destroy the Eklingji temple. As he struck the bull with his sword a swarm of bees flew from inside and attacked him; believing this to be a bad portent, Alaudin left the temple intact. Two other important temples of the Eklingji complex are dedicated to Meerabai, a mystic princess, and Ambika, god of earth.

Prophecy of Sisodia greatness

The temple opening hours are rather strange and are geared to the prayer times: 04.45 to 07.30, 10.30 to 13.30 and 17.30 to 19.45.

A 2 km-walk—or bus or cycle ride—away from Elkingji are the ruins of **Nagda** clustered on the shores of Lake Baghela. Particularly noteworthy are the Vishnu temples of Sas Bahu dating from the 11th C and the 15th C Abdhudji and Parshwanath Jain temples.

Continuing north along the Eklingji road you reach **Haldighati** (40 km from Udaipur), the historic battlefield where Maharana Pratap took on the superior Mughal forces led by Man Singh, the Kuchwaha Rajput. Though Pratap lost the battle and fled the field, Haldighati is a reminder of Rajput resistance. A local guide will show you the memorial dedicated to Chetak, Pratap's horse; the site where the Mughals camped and first fell into conflict with the Rajputs; Rakta Talai where another frenzied encounter took place and the narrow gorge through which Pratap escaped on Chetak. There is a small Tourist Rest House at Haldighati.

Hindu pilgimage

Further on the main route north and 48 km from Udaipur is **Nathdwara** (the Gateway to God), a major centre of pilgrimage. Towards the end of the 17th C Maharana Raj Singh secretly moved the black marble statue of Krishna from the holy city of Mathura, Krishna's birthplace, because he feared Aurangzeb might try and destroy it. The cart carrying the statue to safety got stuck in the sand at the village of Siarh. Believing that this was a sign that Krishna wanted to go no further, the maharana decided to build a temple here and he renamed the village Nathdwara. Today the temple, **Sri Nathji**, is one of the most important Hindu places of worship in Rajasthan. Six times a day, before each of the pujas, the Vaishnite temple priests change the statue's clothes; each period of the day represents a different stage in Krishna's life. And all around Nathdwara you will find shops and kiosks selling model souvenirs of the black Krishna dressed in his various garments. Non-Hindus are not allowed to enter the temple, nevertheless the busy and colourful streetlife of Nathdwara is sufficient compensation for those of a different faith. There are many dharamsalas for the pilgrims and a modest Tourist Bungalow for the tourists.

Beyond, 65 km north of Udaipur where the road forks, one track continuing on to Ajmer and the other to Bhilwara, you come to **Lake Rajsamand** which was created when Maharana Raj Singh dammed the waters of the local river in 1660. It is a pleasant spot with marble terraces and pavilions by the waterfront. Nearby, at **Kankroli**, the Dwarikadheesh temple is an important shrine for Vishnu devotees.

84 km along another road north of Udaipur you arrive at the formidable clifftop **fort of Kumbhal-**

garh, one of the greatest and most historic bastions in Mewar. Built by Maharana Kumbha in the 15th C on a rugged Aravalli clifftop 400 metres above the surrounding plains, Kumbhalgarh symbolizes the Sisodias' defiance of the Mughals. It did not experience the horrific sackings suffered by Chittorgarh, the capital—rather it was a remote stronghold and retreat. A windy road passes through a series of gates on the way up to the castle. At Nimboo Pol there is a shrine to the Mer chief who Rana Kumbha had to defeat before gaining access to the summit. Amongst the *temples* within the fort are the Nilkanth Mahadev with its black marble lingam and the Mata Mandik, a Durga shrine; there are also the tombs of Maharana Kumbha and his grandson, Prithviraj, who was poisoned here by his brother-in-law. A guide will show you the rooms where Udai Singh was raised after he had been smuggled out of Chittorgarh. Up at the top of Kumbhalgarh is the *Badal Mahal*, the Palace of Clouds, which was renovated by Fateh Singh in the last century.

30 km on from Kumbhalgarh is the 15th C **temple of Charbhujaji** which attracts thousands of Hindu pilgrims every month of Bhadrapad Shukla. A short distance beyond, at the village of **Sevantri,** is the larger 14th C **Roopji temple** dedicated to Vishnu. An early maharana was cursed by Lord Roopnarayan and since then no maharana has visited the temple.

Kumbhalgarh Sanctuary is in this region—the nearest town is Sadri, 30 km northwest of Kumbhalgarh. Amongst the game here is the endangered wolf.

Pilgrimage to Ranakpur

Beautiful Jain temple setting

The remarkable **temple complex at Ranakpur**, exquisitely set in a beautiful and isolated Aravalli Valley just west of Kumbhalgarh—though on a different route out of Udaipur—is one of the most important Jain places of worship in the whole of India. A high wall surrounds the main complex and from the outside all you see are the carved domes

Part of the temple complex at Ranakpur

and spires and, if there is a breeze, the long thin banners flapping from their poles.

Construction of Ranakpur commenced in 1446 during the reign of Rana Kumbha. The main temple, **Chaturmukh**, took 50 years to complete and is dedicated to the tirthankar Rishabdeo—though the name is derived from the four-faced white marble image of Adinath in the main sanctum; it is one of the five holiest places for Jains in India. The craftsmanship is outstanding and the ceilings and pillars have been carved in the most minute detail—each one of the 1444 pillars has its own style of decoration.

A short booklet giving a full description of Chaturmukh is available at Ranakpur and there are Jain temple guides to show visitors around. The temple is open to non-Jains between midday and 17.00.

There are two other Jain temples in front of Chaturmukh; the one dedicated to Parsvanath was built in the 14th C and is well known for its erotic carvings.

Most visitors to Ranakpur are Jain pilgrims and there are special dharamsalas and kitchens to accommodate and feed them; there is also a small Tourist Bungalow. Ranakpur is a convenient place to break the journey between Udaipur and Jodhpur. It takes four to six weary hours on a local bus to cover the 96 km, much of it through hills, from Udaipur to Ranakpur. The road continues on to Jodhpur; alternatively there is a railway station at Falna, 37 km west of Ranakpur (it can be reached by bus), which is on the Ajmur-Abu road line.

Excursions South and East of Udaipur

Another famous and ancient Jain temple is at **Rikhabdeo**, 68 km south of Udaipur on the Ahmedabad road. Dating back to the 14th C this ornate shrine to Lord Rishabdeo is also an important place of pilgrimage.

Also south of Udaipur, but on a different road, is **Jaisamand** (48 km from Udaipur)—measuring 15 km by 10 km it is the second largest artificial lake in Asia. Created in the 17th C by Maharana Jai Singh, Jaisamand was a summer retreat and on its shores there are still the summer palaces, terraces, pavilions and neat gardens. Fishing communities live on the small islands in the lake. Jaisamand has simple Tourist Bungalow accommodation.

Jaisamand Wildlife Sanctuary, 8 km from Jaisamand, covers 65 sq km and is the home of panther, leopard, chital, chinkara, antelope, sambar, sloth bear and hyena; the best season is October to June and a Forest Rest House offers simple accommodation. Beyond Jaisamand, near Pratapgarh and 200 km from Udaipur, is the large **Sitamata Sanctuary** where there are leopard, antelope, chinkara, sambar, wild boar and, notably, flying squirrels. There is a DAK Bungalow at Pratapgarh.

Erotic anticlimax

The 10th C **Jagat Ambika Mata temple**, 58 km east of Udaipur, is sometimes dubbed the Kharjuraho of Rajasthan because of its profusion of erotic carvings. Erotic comparisons aside, Jagat may prove to be an anticlimax because of its deteriorated state.

Chittorgarh: Evocation of the Rajput Spirit

On the plateau of a long narrow solitary hill rising 180 metres above the flat plains 112 km northeast of Udaipur stand the ghostly remains of Chittorgarh, the greatest of all Rajasthan's fortified citadels. No other place so evokes the Rajput's spirit of chivalry, courage, romance and passion.

As is the case with places of exceptional greatness, it is assumed that Chittorgarh has mythological origins. And when the realists try to unravel the history they learn that Bappa Rawal, the 8th C Sisodia chief, may have founded this former capital of Mewar or it may have been the 6th C Guhil or an even earlier ancestor; nobody seems to know.

On three historic occasions the Rajput men of Chittorgarh, pitched against superior opposition, donned their saffron robes of martyrdom and fought to their death, while the women mounted huge pyres to perform the inevitable johar. It was every Rajputs' duty—his privileged birthright—to die rather than submit. It was a prescription for doom, for the Rajputs lost thousands of their prize stock every time they flung open their gates to face their ghastly ritual suicide.

After the final sacking in 1568 by Akbar, the Sisodias chose to build a new capital, Udaipur, and when Emperor Jahangir returned Chittorgarh to them in 1616 they did not bother to go back, preferring to leave their abandoned citadel as an empty memorial to their heroic ancestors.

Touring the Abandoned Citadel

Today the deserted and crumbling ruins of **Chittorgarh**, sprawled across an area of 280 hectares, are still enclosed by their sturdy battlements. To the west, immediately below the fort, is the modern town of Chittor. Daily RTDC minibus tours leave from the Tourist Bungalow and they are worth taking because it is a weary trudge wandering around the widely scattered remains and, also, the guide will add a lively history to tumbledown buildings and otherwise meaningless piles of stones.

Touring the citadel

From the eastern edge of town a kilometre-long path snakes its way up through seven gateways. *Padal Pol*, the first gate, is where Prince Bagh Singh was killed during the 1535 sacking of Chittorgarh. The youngsters Jaimal and Kalla, well loved heroes to this day, fell at *Bhairon Pol* while gallantly fighting off Akbar's men in 1568 and there is a shrine to 15-year-old Patta, who also heroically perished in the same conflict, near *Ram Pol*, the final gate.

A small community live within the fort, clustered near the entrance. To the right is the classical Rajput-style **Rana Kumbha's palace**, sadly in a state of deterioration, nevertheless still of historical and architectural interest. You can see the old elephant and horse stables and there is an important Shiva temple within the complex. One of the johars, when thousands of women immolated themselves, is said to have taken place in the vaults of this palace.

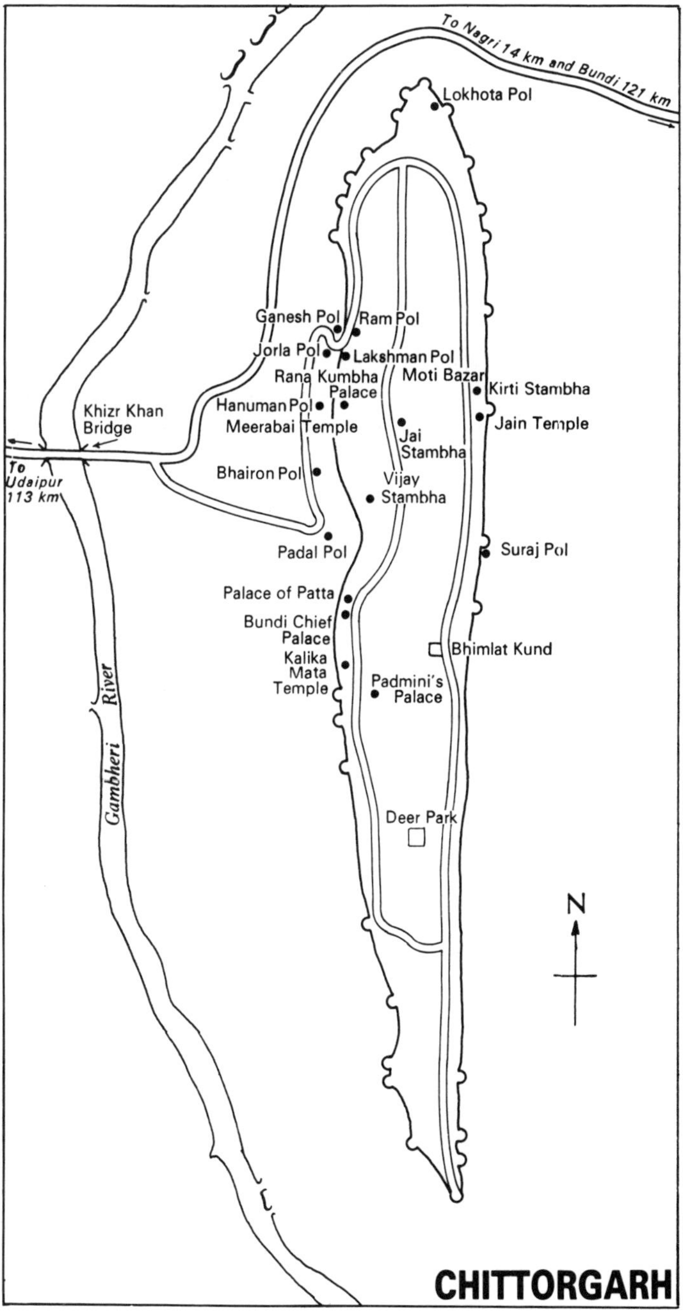
To Nagri 14 km and Bundi 121 km
Lokhota Pol
Ganesh Pol
Ram Pol
Jorla Pol
Lakshman Pol
Rana Kumbha Palace
Moti Bazar
Kirti Stambha
Hanuman Pol
Jain Temple
Meerabai Temple
Jai Stambha
Khizr Khan Bridge
To Udaipur 113 km
Bhairon Pol
Vijay Stambha
Padal Pol
Suraj Pol
Palace of Patta
Bundi Chief Palace
Bhimlat Kund
Kalika Mata Temple
Padmini's Palace
Gambheri River
Deer Park
N
CHITTORGARH

Housed in the nearby **Fateh Prakash Palace**—the palace was built as a private residence by Maharana Fateh Singh in the 1920s—is an interesting *museum* with local archaeological finds, sculptures and weapons associated with the Sisodias. Near to it is the Indo-Aryan style **Meera temple** built in the mid-1400s during the reign of Rana Kumbha and dedicated to the legendary poetess Princess Meerabai who spent all her time venerating a statue of Krishna—and nearby too the larger **Vishnu temple** of Kumbha Shyam.

To the south stands the imposing **Vijay Stambha** or Tower of Victory, one of Rana Kumbha's most impressive and famous constructions. The 37-metre, nine-storey tower was built between 1458 and 1468 to commemorate the Rana's victory over Mahmud Khilji of Malwa and Gujerat in 1440. Numerous small sculptures elaborately decorate the exterior of the tower. For a nominal entrance fee you can climb to the top by means of a rather dark tight internal stairway.

Sati cemetery

In the same quarter of the fort is the **Samdiheshwar Shiva temple** and the **Mahasati**, the place where royalty were cremated and thus, in accordance with old Hindu customs, where their wives came to their end by mounting the funeral pyre and performing sati; you can still see the traditional sati stones with women's handprints. This was also the site of the second johar.

Beyond, at the edge of the cliff, is the deep **Gaumukh reservoir** fed by a spring which spouts through the mouth of a carved cow—hence the name Gaumukh, Mouth of the Holy Cow.

Then on to Padmini's palace. On the way you pass **Patta's palace**, home of young Patta who died after a gallant fight against Akbar's men, and the old 8th C Sun Temple which was converted in the 14th C to the **Kalika Mata temple**—the Mother Goddess temple. It is said that Padmini's beauty was the cause of the first sacking of Chittorgarh and the subsequent johar. **Padmini's palace** still stands overlooking her pool, and a guide will lead

Kirti Stambh—the Tower of Fame—at Chittorgarh

Padmini's johar

you into a chamber and point to a mirror high on the wall in which you can see the reflection of the steps outside leading down to the water's edge. This was how Alaudin, from this spot, saw Padmini as she descended the steps, and entranced by her loveliness took the measures to capture her which ended in the tragic death of thousands of Rajputs. The site of the johar, in which Padmini was the final victim, was in a cavern near the Gaumukh reservoir. Akbar plundered the palace's bronze gates and you can see them now in Agra fort.

South of Padmini's palace you will come to the **deer park**—your guide can also show you the place where the traitors were thrown to their death. But if you double back and continue along the eastern walls of Chittorgarh you will reach the 13th C **Nilkantha Mahadeva temple** enshrining a revered black stone lingam. Nearby is the old citadel's other famous tower, the **Kirti Stambha**, the Tower of Fame. Built in the 12th C by a Jain merchant in honour of Adinath, the first Jain Tirthanker, the Kirti Stambha was the inspiration for Rana Kumbha's Jai Stambha. They are of the same architectural style, though the Kirti Stambha is smaller—only 22 metres and seven storeys high—and the ornate carvings covering the exterior are of the naked figures of the different tirthankars, suggesting that this was a monument for the Digambara—or sky-clad—sect of Jains who go around naked. For a small fee you can climb the cramped stairway to the top of the tower.

In and Around Chittor

There is nothing special about modern **Chittor town**, though the typically colourful back streets near the foot of the hill are of some interest. The bus station is by the river and the Tourist Bungalow and Tourist Office are in the most recent quarter of town which has grown up beyond, around the railway line.

Nagri, 14 km north of Chittor, is one of Rajasthan's oldest towns and it had a thriving Hindu and Buddhist community from the Maurya to Gupta periods; significant archaeological discoveries from this era have been made here.

Just off the main road, about halfway between Chittor and Bundi, stand the remnants of **Mandalgarh**, another of Rana Kumbha's fine castles, and popularly ranked 'Number Three'—after Chittorgarh and Kumbhalgarh—amongst the great forts of Mewar.

PRACTICAL INFORMATION

UDAIPUR

Udaipur, out of all the cities in Rajasthan, offers the most magnificent, opulant and exotic palace hotels.

Best of all is the *Shiv Niwas* (tel: 3236; telex: 033 203 LPAL IN—the same as the Lake Palace Hotel, see below; managing group: Taj Hotels; upper range price bracket; 18 suites), a section of the City Palace with beautiful views over Lake Pichola. The dazzling white marble courtyard is enclosed by the turreted royal suites and apartments, giving guests complete privacy in their enchanted world. The hotel has been tastefully decorated with some of Udaipur's most priceless pieces—the Crystal Room is particularly spectacular. The grander suites are a series of chambers—furnished in traditional styles, but obviously with all mod cons—and can sleep several. However, the cost of staying in the Shiv Niwas, the ultimate and most luxurious palace hotel, is Rs1500–3000 plus.

More famous is the *Lake Palace* (tel: 3241; telex: 033 203 LPAL IN; managing group: Taj Hotels; upper range price bracket; 82 rooms/suites), the brilliant white marble palace standing serenely in the middle of Lake Pichola. The courtyards, one with tumbling bourgainvillea, another with a small marble swimming pool, are lovely quiet spots to while away the hours; that is if the palace is not swarming with tourists (try and avoid the height of the season). The suites are attractively decorated in traditional styles, while most of the 'modern' rooms are rather ordinary. Non-residents may visit the Lake Palace, though they are restricted to certain quarters; the restaurant is open to all. A small motor boat chugs between the City Palace and the Lake Palace.

The grand colonial-style *Laxmi Vilas Palace Hotel* (tel: 4411; managing group; Indian Tourist Development Corporation; upper range price bracket) is the best of the cluster of hilltop hotels overlooking Lake Fateh Sagar; the panoramic view from up here is splendid. The rooms are large, airy and comfortable and without any overt chicness. Next door is the local government-run *Anand Bhawan* (tel: 3256; mid- to upper range price bracket), which also has character and is an interesting place to stay. Nearby you will find the modern and good *Hotel Hill Top* (tel: 3708; mid- to upper range price bracket).

Hotel Lake End (tel: 3841; mid- to upper range price bracket), Alkapuri, down by Lake Fateh Sagar, is large, modern-style, though dated and rather drab. If you are unable to stay at any of the grander palace hotels, but want a hotel with local character and charm, try the *Rang Niwas* (tel: 4923; lower to mid-range price bracket), Lake Palace Road, where the rooms enclose a small and pleasant courtyard. It is a fun place to stay and it is near to Lake Pichola, the City Palace and the old town; other inexpensive lodges have recently opened up nearby.

Back in the newer part of town the *Chandra Lok* (tel: 4558; mid-range price bracket), Saheli Marg, is one of the better modern hotels. The *Kajri Tourist Bungalow* (tel: 3509; mid-range price bracket), Shastri Circle, is centrally located in the modern part of town—as are the following lower range price bracket hotels: the *Alka* (tel: 3611), the *Ashoka* (tel: 3925), the *Prince* (tel: 4355), all in Shastri Circle; and the *Sonike* (tel: 5353), near the bus stand. The *Keerti Hotel* (tel: 3639), Saraswati Marg, is popular with backpacking travellers and is a well known rendezvous amongst them; it is, however, in need of a good clean up. Under the same management as the Keerti is the *Pratap Country Inn*, which is in the country 6 km out of town. Once again it is a meeting point for young independent travellers and you can pitch a tent in the garden, swim in the pool and go for horse rides; it too needs a facelift—maybe this has already been done. Free transport is offered by the boss between the Keerti and the Pratap.

Also out of town, about 3 km, is the *Shikarbadi* (tel: 5321; upper range price bracket; managing group: Oberoi Hotels), an old royal hunting lodge which has been attractively converted into a small hotel. It has a lovely setting on the edge of a lake and forest—away from the downtown bustle and the tourists in the grander palace hotels.

AROUND UDAIPUR

At places like Nathdwara, Eklingji, Haldighati and other important places there are dharamsalas, small government Rest Houses or DAK Bungalows. Consult the Tourist Office for further information.

CHITTORGARH

Of the limited selection of places to stay in Chittor the *Panna Tourist Bungalow* (tel: 274; mid-range price bracket), Udaipur Road, is your best bet. It is amongst the development which has grown up along the railway line on the opposite side of the Gambheri River to the fort and old town. Alternatively try the rather grand *Circuit House* (tel: 277) up the road.

Otherwise you can try the following lower range price bracket accommodation: *Janta Aves Griha* (tel: 9), opposite the railway station and by the Tourist Office; the *Shalimar* (tel: 542), also by the station; and the *Natraj* (tel: 509), by the bus stand. The railway station itself has Retiring Rooms or if you want to be up in the fort there is the simple Birla dharamsala.

THE JODHPUR REGION

The Rathores established themselves in Marwar on the barren eastern edges of the Thar desert. They married into the Sisodia clan and by quirk of inheritance—and a touch of Machiavellian subterfuge—they almost gained the more pleasant lands of Mewar for themselves. But the Sisodias reacted quickly, extinguishing any claims with the necessary violence, and the Rathores slunk back to their desert kingdom. Intrigue and fiery exchanges between the Rajput families were all too frequent in medieval times. Marwar itself was not regarded as a big enough prize by most of the local superpowers and so the Rathores were able to consolidate their city state more or less unmolested and by the time they were attacked they were able to resist their aggressors. The Rathores did join the Mughal fold and typically the emperors gave them roles to play in the empire. However, the Rathore–Mughal bond was often turbulent and there was an underlying distrust between the two households: the Rathores viewed the Mughals with contempt, while the Mughals treated the Rathores with suspicion.

The Rathores of Marwar

In 1193 Mohammed Ghori, flushed after his victory over Prithviraj Chauhan at the Battle of Tarain near Delhi, pushed further east and overran the kingdom of Kanauj—the lands on the River Ganges east of Agra. The local king, Jaichand, was killed—'he met a death congenial to the Hindu, being drowned in the sacred stream [the Ganges] in attempting to escape' (Tod)—but a group of his descendants fled and migrated west, eventually settling in the harsh and barren lands of Marwar, the 'Region of Death', in the Thar desert.

Seoji, one of Jaichand's grandsons, won substantial territories, though it was not until the end of the 14th C when Chunda captured Mandore, the capital of the Parihar tribe, and married a local prin-

A woman of Jodhpur

cess, that the Rathore dynasty began to emerge as a prominant Rajput clan.

Chunda's daughter, Hansa, married Rana Lakha of Mewar and thus the Rathore and Sisodia families were linked. The relationship was further consolidated when the couple had a son, Mokul, though complications arose five years later when the rana died and the gaadi was open to contention.

Here was the chance of Rao Rinmull, Chunda's son and successor, 'who deemed the region of Maroo-des [Marwar], and its rabri, or maize porridge, well exchanged for the fertile plains and wheaten bread of Mewar' (Tod), to take advantage of his young nephew Mokul's inheritance and herald the lad as the new Rana of Mewar.

Fearing such intrigues, the Sisodias launched a surprise attack on the Rathores as they feasted at Gasconda, 10 km south of Chittorgarh:

Love, wine, opium and death

'The guards at the gates were cut to pieces, and the Rathore hunted out and killed without mercy. The end of Rinmull was more ludicrous than tragic. Smitten with the charms of a Sisodia handmaid of the queen, who was compelled to his embrace, the old chief was in her arms, intoxicated with love, wine, and opium, and heard nothing of the tumult without. A woman's wit and revenge combined to make his end afford some compensation for her loss of honour. Gently rising, she bound him to his bed with his own Marwari turban (often sixty cubit lengths): nor did this disturb him, and the messengers of fate had entered ere the opiate allowed his eyes to open to a sense of his danger. Enraged, he in vain endeavoured to extricate himself, and by some tortuosity of movement he got upon his legs, his wallet at his back like a shell or shield of defence. With no arms but a brass vessel of ablution, he levelled to the arch several of his assailants, when a ball from a matchlock extended him on the floor of the palace. His son Joda was in the lower town, and was indebted to the fleetness of his steed for escaping the fate of his father and kindred, whose bodies strewed the terre-pleine of Cheetore, the merited reward of their usurption and treachery' (Tod).

Joda returned to Marwar as Rinmull's successor and on the advice of a local ascetic he abandoned Mandore, founding in 1459 a new capital on a solitary craggy hill not far to the south. This he named Jodhpur after himself. It was a time of expansion for the Rathores—their domain stretched to over 200,000 sq km—but the prolificacy of their raos (Chunda had 14 sons, Rinmull 24 sons and Joda 14 sons) meant that the lands had to be divided amongst an ever increasing number of princes. For this reason, Bika, one of Joda's sons, set off to colonise his own territories (see Bikaner).

Maldeo was proclaimed rao in 1532, five years after the Rajput forces under Rana Sanga of Mewar had been defeated by Barbur the Mughal at the Battle of Kanauj. After Kanauj, Barbur virtually ignored the deserts of Rajputana, preferring to concentrate his attention on the more fruitful plains of the Ganges. At this time the Sisodias were at a low ebb, smarting from the wounds inflicted by their various enemies and from their own ritual suicides in the form of johars which had decimated their population. Maldeo, 'the most valiant and energetic Rajpoot of his time' (Tod), took full advantage of the situation to consolidate his own Rathore kingdom.

When Sher Shah turned his aggression towards the arid lands of Marwar, Maldeo forced him to retreat back to Delhi—the emperor poignantly exlaimed afterwards that 'he had nearly lost the empire of Hindust'han for a handful of barley'—and later Akbar was only able to keep Maldeo in check by fostering rivalry between the Jodhpur and Bikaner clans of Rathores.

Mughal supremacy

However, the last years of Maldeo's reign were as lacking in lustre as his former years were glorious, and the aging rao finally conceded to Mughal supremacy by allowing his eldest son Udai Singh to go and pay homage to Akbar in Delhi. And on succeeding his father Udai Singh gave his daughter's hand in marriage to the emperor as a gesture of friendship.

Udai Singh suffered a strange fate: 'Although he had no less than 27 queens, he cast the eye of desire on a virgin daughter of a subject and that subject a Brahmin' (Tod). The Brahmin father chose to kill his daughter rather than let her marry Udai Singh, a man of a different caste; he cut her up and burnt her and as the flames leapt he cried: 'Let peace be a stranger to him [Udai Singh]! And in three pahars [a period of about three hours], three days and three years, let me have my revenge'. He then threw himself on the pyre. This incident was related to Udai Singh and it haunted him until he died at the very time which had been foretold by the Brahmin.

Marwar prospered as long as it remained on good terms with the Mughals. In 1638 Jaswant Singh, the great grandson of Udai Singh, became rao. He was, according to local folklore, 'unequalled amongst the princes of his time. Stupidity and ignorance were banished; and science flourished where he ruled; many were the books composed under his auspices'.

Jaswant Singh served brilliantly in Shah Jahan's army, but he got tangled up in the Mughal battle for succession, picking the losing side by opting to support Dara against his brother Aurangzeb. On becoming emperor, Aurangzeb unsuccessfully tried to woo Jaswant Singh, but eventually had to be content with giving him governorships of obscure outposts to keep him out of harm's way. Jaswant 'detested the whole race [Moslems] inimical to the religion and independence of his own'. If he had been able to secure the help of other Rajputs he would almost certainly have overthrown Aurangzeb, but the clans were unable to unite successfully and Jaswant ultimately 'prefered hollow submission better than avowed hostility' (Tod). Jaswant saw out his final days as the governor of Kabul. A sad man, he had seen two sons die in Kabul and his heir—his only other male issue—had been poisoned by Aurangzeb. His death in 1681 was a relief to Augangzeb, as 'sighs never ceased flowing from Aurangzeb's heart while Jaswant lived' (Tod).

Jaswant's wife was dissuaded from becoming sati because she was pregnant and instead the rao's other queen and seven concubines burned on the pyre. On the return from Kabul to Jodhpur, Jaswant's posthumous son and successor, Ajit, was born, but the convoy was stopped by Aurangzeb's men who demanded the child. The Rathores refused to hand him over and, having smuggled him out of the camp, the men fought to their death and the women went into a room, filled it with gunpowder and then lit the fuse. Durga Das, a Rathore noble, took Ajit to the safety of a mountain retreat at Abu.

This was a period of great hostility between Aurangzeb and the Rajputs. Imperial forces poured into Rajputana: 'Rapine and conflagration spread over the land. The country became a waste; fear stalked triumphant' (Tod).

For almost 30 years Durga Das fought tirelessly against Aurangzeb for Marwar's independence and finally in 1709, two years after the emperor's death, he entered Jodhpur and put Ajit on the gaadi. As a Rajput his conduct had been exemplary. Tod fittingly commented: 'What a splendid example is the heroic Durga Das of all that constitutes the glory of the Rajpoot. Valour, loyalty, integrity, combined with prudence in all difficulties which surround him, are qualities which entitle him to admiration which his memory continues to enjoy'.

Jodhpur

Founding of Jodhpur

Mandore was too exposed to attack and so in 1459, on the advice of a hermit, Jodha built a citadel, Meharangarh, on top of the nearby Bukurcheerea, the Birds' Nest, a sheer 125-metre rock. Jodha built his new capital round its base and named it after himself. The fort's honey-coloured walls look as if they rise straight from the cliff face and the dramatic setting, overlooking miles of flat, empty, dusty plains, is as imposing as that of any castle in Rajasthan.

'... A projecting elevation on the same range on which Mandore was placed, and about four miles south of it. Doubtless its inaccessible position seconded the recommendation of the hermit, for its scarped summit renders it almost impregnable, while its superior elevation permits the sons of Jodha to command, from the windows of their palace, a range of vision almost comprehending the limits of their sway. In clear weather, they can view the summits of their southern barrier, the gigantic Aravulli; but in every other direction, it fades away in the boundless expanse of sandy plains' (Tod).

Jodhpur was built around the foot of the Bakurcheerea and was later enclosed by the 10-km wall which still demarks the old town from the new. In those belligerent days it must have been extremely comforting for the inhabitants to be able to look up at the Meharangarh, the Majestic Fort, standing high and dominant in the centre of their town protecting all those who lived in its shadows.

Exploring Jodhpur's 'Majestic Fort'

A steep windy road leads from the town up to **Meharangarh**—there is a longer though gentler route via Jaswant Thada. Pock-marked by cannonball fire, *Jayapol*, the first of a series of huge impressive gates, was built by Rao Man Singh in 1806 to commemorate his success over the Jaipur and Bikaner forces. *Fatehpol*, Victory Gate, stands as a tribute to Ajit Singh's victory over the Mughals in 1707 and by the last gate, *Lohapol*, Iron Gate, started by Maldeo the 16th C Rathore hero and completed in the 18th C, are the dozen or so sati handprints serving as evocative epitaphs to the wives of Man Singh who burnt on their husband's funeral pyre in 1843.

The delicate palaces within

In sharp contrast to the formidable fortifications of the exterior, which must have deterred many a would-be attacker, are the delicately carved sandstone screens enclosing the palaces within the fort.

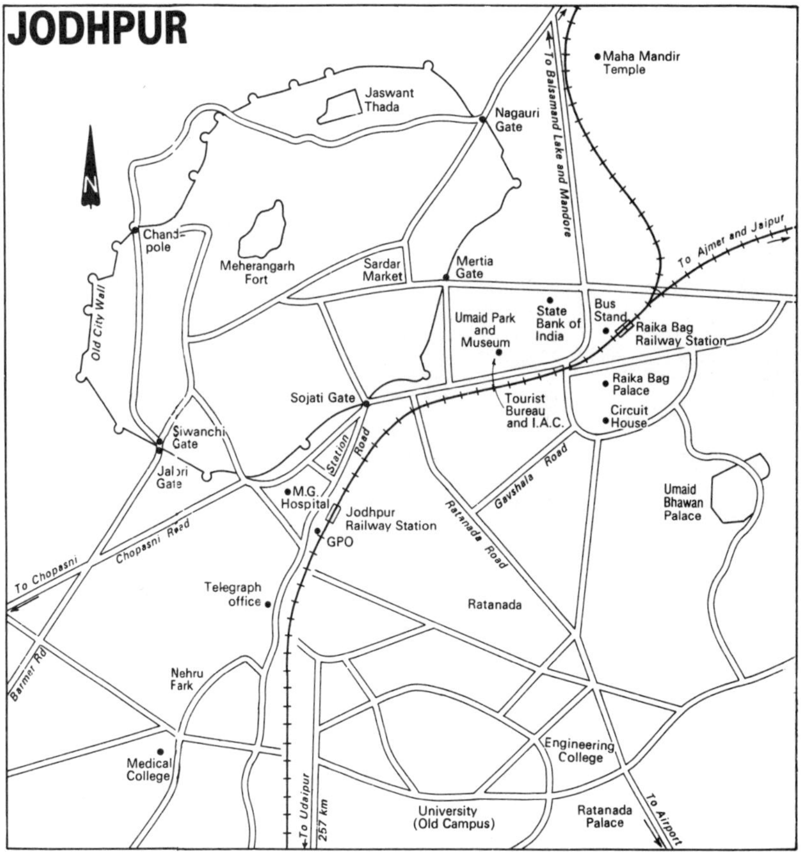

While the outside tells about the Rajput as a man of war, the interior gives an insight into the other side of his character. The royal apartments—such as **Sukh Mahal** (Pleasure Palace), **Moti Mahal** (Pearl Palace), **Phool Mahal** (Flower Palace)—are open to the public and conjure up the spirit of the indulgent regal past. They show that the Rajput loved fantastic pomp, enjoyed good times and was a great patron of the arts. There is a marvellous collection of palaquins, elephant howdahs—used by the raos when they sat in all their glory atop their elephants and paraded through the

The fort at Jodhpur, forbidding from the outside but enclosing delicate palaces within

streets below—and even a display of royal babies' cradles.

You are shown former raos' chambers and the office of one of their prime ministers which has been maintained as it was when in use. Exquisite Rajputana miniature paintings, local musical instruments, ornate pieces of furniture from around the world and the weapons and costumes brandished and worn by the old Rathore heroes are all on display.

The view from the Bird's Nest

Outside the complex of palaces—they are as lovely and fascinating as any you will see in Rajasthan—you are back with the more practical side of defence. The old cannons still poke through the battlements at the southern end of the fort. The **panorama** is stunning; indeed, Tod's impression that Meharangarh's 'superior elevation permits the sons of Jodha to command, from the windows of their palace, a range of vision almost comprehending the limits of their sway', was probably not much of an exaggeration. Directly below clusters the tightly packed town. You can see all the action in the streets, hear the general hub-bub and by allowing yourself a little sensory licence you will catch a whiff of the smells. At Jodhpur's eastern limits you can discern the distinctive silhouette of Umaid Bhawan Palace—a more recent palace and now a hotel—and to the west of the Bakurcheerea many of the houses are painted blue which is traditionally the colour of Brahmin residences.

Meharangarh opening times are 08.00 to 18.00 (March to August) and 09.00 to 17.00 (September to February).

A short walk north of Meharangarh—and also with a good view of the city—is **Jaswant Thada**, the rather grand white marble memorial (the marble was brought from the Markrana quarries 240 km from Jodhpur) built in 1899 to commemorate Rao Jaswant Singh II. This was where royalty were cremated. Hanging inside are portraits of erstwhile rulers and outside, within the confines of the split level black and white tiled chequer board courtyard, are the cenotaphs to other past raos. Opening times are 08.00 to 18.00.

Down Below

Jodhpur itself has no other outstanding sights, though as with so many towns much of its charm lies in its street life. A good starting point for wanders is the Clock Tower and the maze of surrounding lanes which make up **Sardar Market**, lively and colourful. There is an assortment of different bazaars specialising in spices and herbs, fruit and vegetables, cloth, silverware and handicrafts and the more prosaic domestic utensils. The best time to visit the market is between 08.30 and midday and from 16.30 to 18.30.

Street life

Outside the limits of the old city walls modern Jodhpur has had a chance to spread itself. It is surrounded by empty desert though the very harshness of these lands is a constraint to further expansion. The **Government Museum** in the pretty

Jaswant Thada at Jodhpur, memorial to royalty

Umaid Gardens houses a collection of a dull and dusty ethnographical and archaeological displays; however there are a few odd relics from the days of the Raj which may give colour to a tour of the museum for the casual visitor. Opening times are 10.00 to 16.30 (closed Fridays and national holidays). There is a small **zoo** near the museum.

Umaid Bhawan, the large domed palace fashioned from the famous Marwar Chittar rose sandstone, was commissioned by Rao Umaid Singh in 1929. Completed in 1943, the palace is grand and imposing in size, but its spacious echoing interior has an atmosphere of restraint and sobriety, especially when compared to the touch of flamboyance you see up at the palaces of Meharangarh. Umaid Bhawan is nevertheless a magnificent place to stay and it is one of the most splendid and palatial of Rajasthan's Palace hotels. It has a small museum of hunting trophies, memorabilia, watches and books which is open to non-residents between 09.00 and 17.00.

Outside Jodhpur

A road leads north out of Jodhpur to Mandore. On the outskirts of town you pass the small walled town of **Mahamandir**, the Great Temple, which was built in 1812 by Rao Man Singh in honour of his guru, Deva. The 84-pillared temple, know as the 100 pillared temple, has paintings depicting various yoga positions.

Continuing along the road you come to the **summer palace of Balsamand**—there is a turning 7 km from Jodhpur and the palace is a few kilometres down this track—which is surrounded by parkland and overlooks an artificial lake originally created in 1159. The palace was built as recently as 1936 and is now in the hands of the local civil service and is not open to the public. The gardens, though, can be visited between 08.00 and 18.00 and they are a popular picnic spot with people from Jodhpur.

On to **Mandore**, 9 km from Jodhpur, the old Rathore capital which was founded by the Pratiharas in the 6th/7th C AD on a rocky plateau. It now lies in ruins largely because Jodha dismantled buildings so he could use the stone in the construction of his new capital. The main attraction here today are the pleasant **gardens** below, where peacocks strut dignifiedly around the neat lawns in true Rajasthani style and a mischievous bunch of monkeys dart between the trees. The gardens at Mandore are a memorial to the past rulers and heroes of Marwar: there are the *cenotaphs* of Maldeo, Jaswant Singh I and, most impressive of all, the red sandstone tomb of Rao Ajit Singh, Jaswant's posthumous son. In the **Hall of Heroes** figures representing heroes and deities have been carved out of the rock face and painted in typically garish colours, and the shrine of 330 million gods, though not enshrining as many effigies, does nevertheless indicate how populous the Hindu pantheon is.

Shrine of 330 million gods

Some of the Jodhpur buses continue from Mandore on to **Osian**, a further 56 km to the north, which was a significant centre of Hinduism and Jainism in the Pratihara and Chauhan periods. The remains of this 8th to 11th C settlement lie in an attractive, isolated, semi-arid desert valley. A cluster of temples still stand— most impressive are the **Sun Temple**, the **Mahavira Temple** and the **Sachiya Temple**. Locals from the village will act as guides around the deserted ruins.

PRACTICAL INFORMATION

JODHPUR

Jodhpur offers its visitors a couple of splendid palace hotels, a fairly new first class hotel and the usual, more ordinary, selection of lesser accommodation.

In 1929 Rao Umaid Singh commissioned his new palace on Chittar Hill—an auspicious site according to the ascetics, though as it was an out of the way location and with no convenient source of water it did seem a rather foolhardy place to build. And from afar, through the hazy sky, the imposing domed silhouette of the *Umaid Bhawan Palace* (tel: 22316; telex: 0352 202 UBP IN; managing group: Welcomgroup Hotels; 55 rooms/suites; upper range price bracket), standing on its slight perch on the eastern outskirts of town, looks a bit like a grand folly.

The Umaid Bhawan was designed by Lanchester, president of the Royal Institute of Architects, in a style akin to the Lutyen's buildings in Delhi and it took tens of thousands of labourers 15 years—a period blighted by famine—to complete the sombre red sandstone palace. Part of the palace remains the residence of the ex-royals, another section is an interesting museum full of family heirlooms, while the rest is a fine hotel. The spirit of the past—'those glorious days of Maharajas and the British Raj' which guests are so keen to experience—and the quirky styles and decor have been tastefully retained while incorporating modern facilities.

Much more modest, less formal, and possibly a lot more fun, is the *Ajit Bhawan* (tel: 20409; 25 rooms; mid-range price bracket), Airport Road, in a leafy quarter of town. A branch of the former royal family have turned their relatively small palace into a glorified guest house. The atmosphere is easy going and homely—casual though elaborate dinners are taken with the family—and the main building is charmingly decorated with memorabilia while the out cottages (self-contained units with private bathrooms) have been tastefully furnished in a local style. The Ajit Bhawan offers excursions and safaris, on camel or by jeep, into the surrounding countryside.

Jodhpur's fairly new and good *Ratanada International* (tel: 25910; upper range price bracket) is a little out-of-town, about ½ km from the airport.

The *Ghoomar Tourist Bungalow* (tel: 21900; mid-range price bracket), High Court Road, and the *Circuit House* (tel: 20999), near Raika Bagh, have pleasant and central locations.

The cheaper lower range price bracket accommodation is around the main railway station and Sojati Gate and includes the *Adarsh Niwas* (tel: 26936), the *Agarwal Lodge* (tel: 20837), the *Arun Hotel* (tel: 20238), the *Galaxy* (tel: 25098) and the *Shanti Bhawan Lodge* (tel: 21689).

KHIMSAR

A part of the fort at Khimsar, 100 km north of Jodhpur on the way to Bikaner, has recently opened as the *Royal Castle Hotel* (tel: 72314; upper range price bracket; managing group: Welcomgroup Hotels; 10 rooms); reservations can be made at the Umaid Bhawan.

THE BIKANER REGION

As ruling clans grew in size in every generation the demand by young princes for new territories increased. Hence Bika, one of the many sons of Jodha, the Rathore king of Marwar, pushed north and colonised the vast arid tracts of northern Rajputana. His own dynastic branch of Rathores consolidated their state and were later party to Akbar's scheme of intermarriage between Mughals and Rajputs. Bikaner, rather out on a limb in a bleak corner of Rajputana, was not one of the foremost Rajput states. However, inspired leadership can suddenly change the fortunes of any kingdom and it was when the motivated Ganga Singh developed revolutionary agricultural schemes, local communications and town planning earlier this century that Bikaner reached its zenith and was regarded as one of the most enlightened of India's princely states.

The Rathores of Bikaner

Bika, the sixth son of Rao Jodha, pushed north from Mandore in 1459—the same year his father founded his new capital of Jodhpur—with the intent of carving out his own territories elsewhere in the Thar Desert. He and his 300 followers fought off opposition and eventually settled amongst a community of resolute Jat farmers in the region of Jangledesh—the northern Thar. Bika received their co-operation in return for providing them with protection against their rivals and a pact was reached whereby Naira, the Jat leader, allowed Bika to build a city. In recognition of this allegiance Bika named his capital Bikaner, after himself and Naira.

By the time Bika died in 1495 the various Rathore clans controlled most of the northern Thar desert and they continued to respect the rights of the Jats —at least until the reign of Rae Singh, Bika's great grandson, who came to the gaadi in 1573: 'Until [Rae Singh's] reign, the Jats had, in a great degree, preserved their ancient privileges. Their mainten-

Women carrying water in the arid Bikaner region

ance was, however, found rather inconvenient, by the now superabundant Rajpoot population, and they were consequently dispossessed of all political authority. With the loss of independence their military spirit decayed, and they sank to mere tillers of the earth' (Tod).

Under Rae Singh, Bikaner rose to become one of the foremost Rajput states. Rae Singh established close links with Emperor Akbar (both were married to sister princesses of Jaisalmer) and, as Tod scornfully commented, 'if the Jats parted with their liberties to the Rajpoot, the latter in like manner, bartered his freedom to become a Satrap of Delhi'. Rae Singh served the Mughals loyally on the battlefield and Akbar reinforced the kinship bond by marrying his son, Salim, to the Rajput's daughter Purvez. Rae Singh died in 1632 and he is most affectionately remembered as the founder of Junagarh, the massive fort around which modern Bikaner grew.

Desert Fortress City

Founded by a splinter group of the Rathores of Marwar in 1489, Bikaner is one of the major fortified cities in the Thar desert and, like Jaisalmer, it was an important market town and stopping point along the caravan routes between northern India and markets to the west and south.

Local hero

One of Bikaner's most prominent rulers was Ganga Singh, who became rao in 1894 when he was only seven years old. During his reign of 46 years he did much to modernise Bikaner—he initiated a huge irrigation programme to combat drought and constructed an extensive railway system to connect his capital and provincial towns with Jaipur and Delhi—and he was also a highly respected statesman in the national forum. For many a Bikaneri Ganga Singh is still a well loved father figure and his name constantly crops up in conversation and is associated with museums, schools, building developments and other public works.

Unlike most of Rajasthan's great forts the

Sati hands at Bikaner fort

immense **Junagarh** does not stand on a commanding hill site, rather it is built on a slight elevation and is surrounded by a wide, deep moat. Enclosed within the thick kilometre-long wall is the usual collection of small palaces, audience halls, gracious courtyards and royal chambers and here at Bikaner, in common with the other desert forts, there is a profusion of finely crafted sandstone latticed screens and windows.

Entrance is through *Karen Pol*, then *Daulat Pol* (here you see sati hands imprinted on the wall) and *Suraj Pol*, the Sun Gate, which is flanked by two huge statues of elephants.

Guided through the palace labyrinth

A guide will lead you through the labyrinth of splendid **palace halls** which have typically evocative names such as *Chandra Mahal* (Moon Palace) and *Phool Mahal* (Flower Palace). The intricate mirror work and fine paintings may now look a bit jaded, but it does not require much imagination to appreciate the opulence and grandeur which once filled the palace.

They used to celebrate the festival of Holi with characteristic frivolity in the large *Durgar Niwas courtyard* and formal functions would take place in the nearby *Anup Mahal*, the huge Coronation Hall. Ganga Singh's study is much as it was during his lifetime; there is the inevitable armoury and an excellent library of Sanskrit and Persian manuscripts.

Junagarh's opening times are 09.30 to 17.00.

Walking Around Bikaner

The **Ganga Golden Jubilee Museum**, one of Rajasthan's better museums, houses a good selection of the usual type of exhibits: the archaeological finds date from pre-Harrapan times and there are also Gupta pieces (4th to 8th C AD) and other pottery and terracottas; there is an excellent collection of miniature paintings from the celebrated 18th C

Lalgarh at Bikaner

Bikaner school (permission is required from the curator to see some of the galleries); a section on the history of Bikaner displays the various possessions of past local heroes (a hall is devoted to Ganga Singh) and the armoury includes a selection of European firearms. Opening times are 10.00 to 17.00 (winter) and 07.30 to 10.30 and 15.30 to 18.00 (summer); closed Fridays and national holidays.

The site of the old fort, **Bika ji-ki-Tekri**, is in the southwest of Bikaner, though there is not much to see today; the *cenotaphs* of Rao Bika and some of the other early rulers are here.

Also in this quarter of the city you will find a cluster of important temples—the **Laxmi Nath Temple** and the **Chintamani Jain Temple**, both dating from the 16th C, and the **Bhandasar Jain Temple** well known locally for its fine carvings. It is believed that Akbar gave Rao Rae Singh a thousand valuable statues in gratitude for conquering Sirohi in southern Rajasthan and it is said that this horde is stashed away under the Chintamani Temple.

Ganga Singh built his vast red sandstone **palace of Lalagarh** in honour of his father Lal Singh. Despite the marvellous craftsmanship—there is a mass of beautifully carved screens—and the grand and majestic proportions of the palace, the formal British Raj influenced design of Lalagarh has given the place an air of austerity. A section of the palace is still the home of the erstwhile royal family and another quarter has been converted into a charming *museum* full of family memorabilia. As usual there are hunting trophies and a series of photos show Ganga Singh shooting five tigers in the space of three minutes. The rest of the palace is a hotel.

Excursions from Bikaner

Bikaner's cluster of *royal cenotaphs* is 8 km east of town by the **Devi Kund Sagar**, an attractive tank.

In the flat dusty scrublands 10 km to the south-east is the only **camel breeding farm** in Asia. Half of India's 1.5 million camels are found in Rajasthan and the Bikaneri breed is particularly hardy and constitutes 50 percent of India's camels and a further 25 percent of her crossbreeds. Indeed, in the First World War Britain had a Bikaneri camel corp. The farm was established in the 1950s and is now home for between 150 and 200 camels. It has an allocation of 8000 hectares for grazing and a modest, though interesting, laboratory. You can visit the farm and see the staff go through their daily routine—they may even give you a camel ride, or at least a glass of fresh camel's milk.

Camels bred

The family of a dead boy brought their son's body to Karni Devi, a famous 15th C mystic with supernatural powers, with the hope that she could bring him back to life. Karni Devi appealed to Lord Yama, God of the Dead, but he refused to resurrect the boy. Furious, Karni Devi proclaimed that she would prefer the dead to be reincarnated as rats for one life rather than pass before Lord Yama. Hence today rats are venerated at the **Karni Mata Temple** at **Deshnok**, 30 km south of Bikaner, and they run around quite freely. If a person acciden-

Rats venerated

tally stamps on a sacred rat and kills it, he is expected to donate a silver or gold model of a rat to the temple priest as a form of penance. The temple's silver gates were given by Ganga Singh.

The **Gajner Sanctuary**, a pleasant wooded area in the desert scrub 32 km southwest of Bikaner, was once the hunting grounds of Ganga Singh. The royal lodge, overlooking a lake, is sometimes used as a hotel and is particularly popular with bird watchers because, amongst other migratory birds, this is the winter home of the imperial Siberian grouse. The animals at Gajner include black buck, nilgai and chinkara.

Kodamdesar, 24 km to the west of Bikaner, is famous for its **Bhaironji Temple**, built by Rao Bika, and the annual festival held here every August.

Thousands of black buck roam the empty saline flatlands about 100 km east of Bikaner. There is a small lodge within the **Tal Chapper Sanctuary**.

PRACTICAL INFORMATION

BIKANER

Ganga Singh's Lalagarh Palace is now a hotel, though as yet it does not rank amongst the top palace hotels. The Tourist Bungalow and cheap lodges offer alternative accommodation.

The large *Lalagarh Palace Hotel* (tel: 3263; upper range price bracket) is just out of town. There are plans to spruce it up, but at present it remains a delightful rambling pile, where the rooms are simply decorated with some fine old pieces and many of the fixtures and fittings date from the palace's earliest days. The bare ballroom, measuring some 30 metres by 15 metres by 12 metres high, is now like a huge hollow vault and the enormous indoor marble swimming pool lies empty. Part of the hotel is still a private residence, while another section is a museum.

The *Dhola Maru Tourist Bungalow* (tel: 5002; mid range price bracket), Puran Singh Circle, is in a newer part of town, though not that far from Junagarh Fort; nearby is the *Circuit House* (tel: 3142). Bottom end of the market accommodation—all lower range price bracket—can be found in Station Road and includes the *Green Hotel* (tel: 3396) and the *Deluxe Hotel* (tel: 3292); the *Vishnoi Dharamsala* (tel: 3278) is in the main park.

GAJNER

The royal family's turn of the century *country retreat* at Gajner (mid range price bracket), 32 km southwest of Bikaner, has been converted into a 'part time' hotel and it is a pleasant place to spend a day or two. Reservations should be made at the Lalagarh Palace.

THE JAISALMER REGION

According to local belief all action and events are destined. The creation and subsequent history of Jaisalmer as forecast by a lone and aged ascetic to the Bhatti king is typically fabulous, but aptly so, for Jaisalmer in reality is an extraordinary place. The Bhattis built up their far flung city state into a defiant Rajput desert outpost, and the tales of their noble fight to uphold family integrity when confronted with the enemy are as splendid as those found in the annals of the Sisodia clan. Finally, though, the Bhattis made peace with Akbar and with subsequent stability Jaisalmer, a market town on one of the old trans-Asian caravan routes, prospered. An influential merchant class evolved under the ruling Bhattis and, indeed, there were long periods when they pulled the strings of power.

The Bhattis of Jaisalmer

The Bhattis settled in the Thar desert in the 8th/9th C after being pushed across the Indus River and then out of Punjab by early waves of Moslem invaders. At the beginning of the 10th C they conquered Ludruvah, but it proved too susceptable to attacks and in the 12th C Rawal Jaisal sought a location for a new city.

Rivers of blood prophecy

During his search Jaisal came across Eesal, a hermit living at the foot of the three-peaked hill, who related the tale of Kak, an ascetic who lived next to the stream at this spot during the ancient 'silver age' and who had once been visited by Lord Krishna and Arjuna. The waters were unclean so Krishna struck the ground with his sword and the stream turned sweet. He went onto prophesy that in the future a city would be built on the three-peaked hill. Having related this tale Eesal concluded by saying that the fields west of the hill should always bare his name (even today they are referred to as the fields of Eesal) and that the city would be twice and a half times sacked; that rivers of blood would flow, and that for a time all would be lost to its descendants.

In 1155 Jaisal lay the foundations of Jaisalmer on the rocky three-peaked hill and, indeed, Eesal's predictions came true.

Jaetsi—the fifth rewal after Jaisal and son of Rawal Lakhun Singh, the simpleton who had ordered quilted jackets for the jackels, as he believed they howled at night because they were cold—came to the throne in 1276. During his reign Alaudin invaded north India and Rajasthan and his forces pushed over to the western Thar and besieged Jaisalmer.

Jaetsi died in 1294 and was succeeded by Moolraj III, who saw no chance of victory against the Moslems and eventually chose to sound the johar. As Tod writes Moolraj announced his decision to his Rajput chiefs and then with Ruttun, his next in command, he 'repaired to the palace of queens. They told them to take the sohag (*sohagun*, one who becomes sati previous to her lord's death), and prepare to meet in heaven, while they gave up their lives in defence of their honour and their faith. Smiling, the Soda Rani, replied, "This night we shall prepare, and by the morning's light we shall be inhabitants of swerga" (heaven); and thus it was with the chiefs and all their wives. The night was passed together for the last time in preparation for the awful morn. It came; ablutions and prayers were finished, and at the Rajdwara (royal gate) were convened bala, prude, and bridu (women of under sixteen, middle age and over forty respectively). They bade a last farewell to all their kin; the johar commenced, and twenty-four thousand females, from infancy to old age, surrendered their lives, some by the sword, other in the volcano of fire. Blood flowed in torrents, while the smoke of the pyre ascended to the heavens; not one feared to die, every valuable was consumed with them, not the worth of a straw was preserved for the foe. This work done, the brothers looked upon the spectacle with horror. Life was now a burden, and they

Mass immolation

A man of the desert

prepared to quit it. They purified themselves with water, paid adoration to the divinity, made gifts to the poor, placed a branch of tulsi (a plant) in their casques, the saligram (a symbolic stone) round their neck; and having cased themselves in armour and put on the saffron robe, they bound the mor (the crown worn by a Rajput chief only at the time of his marriage and when he is going to die in battle) around their heads, and embraced each other for the last time. Thus they awaited the hour of battle. Three thousand eight hundred warriors, with faces red with wrath, prepared to die with their chiefs.'

The victorious Moslems stationed a contingent of soldiers at Jaisalmer, but they had little use for this ghostly and far off citadel and eventually they abandoned the place.

Around the turn of the 14th C Rawal Doodoo reoccupied Jaisalmer; he extended the Bhatti's boundaries and went on to challenge the Moslems at Ajmer. The Moslems retaliated by attacking Jaisalmer and this resulted in the city's second sacking.

The half johar occurred in the 16th C when Amir Ali, a Pathan, besieged Jaisalmer. Lunkeran, the incumbent rawal, expected defeat and, having slain his princesses with his own sword, he went on to fight the customary battle to the death. However he won and the event is classified as a half johar partly because Lunkeran was victorious and partly because the women died by sword rather than immolation.

Relics of prosperity

In 1570 Rawal Hari Singh gave one of his daughters in marriage to Akbar, hence uniting his Bhatti clan with the Mughals. In the 17th C the Bhattis rose to prominence and over the following centuries Jaisalmer became an increasingly important market place for long distance caravans travelling between India and central Asia. Trade flourished and the prosperous merchants built for themselves splendid havelis—mansions magnificently crafted from the local honey-coloured sandstone. The old camel trails died out as the new sea

The medieval walls of Jaisalmer rise above the Thar Desert

routes from the port of Bombay took over the trade and many of the important mercantile families, now redundant in Jaisalmer, moved to the large cities to continue their business; their deserted havelis still stand as a testimony to their affluence.

Jaisalmer: the Citadel

Isolated in the flat dusty empty tracts of the Thar, far in the west of Rajasthan, rises the medieval walled city of **Jaisalmer** carved from golden sandstone. Founded in the 12th C Jaisalmer was the distant capital of the Bhatti clan of Rajputs and an oasis (the final syllable, *mer*, means rocky oasis) for travellers to this bleak corner of the desert. It is still today one of the remotest—and most exotic—cities in India, and the old saying warned:

Horse of wood
Legs of stone
A frame of iron
Will get you to Jaisalmer alone.

Jaisalmer's strategic position close to the Pakistan

border was highlighted during the Indo-Pakistan wars of 1965 and 1971. Hence a railway and proper roads were laid to Jaisalmer, connecting it to other centres in Rajasthan and the rest of India. There remains a military presence in Jaisalmer.

Oldest of Rajasthan's major towns, Jaisalmer remains marvellously preserved within its ancient solid walls. The city has developed outside, but the majority of the 20,000 or so population live within, in the enclosed area which covers some 8 sq km.

Jaisalmer is dominated by its heavily fortified **citadel** which was built by Jaisal on top of the 80-metre high Trikuta hill. Entrance is through a typically formidable series of *gates*—Suraj Pol, Bhuta Pol, Ganesh Pol, Hawa Pol—and on the way up you can see *Krishna's umbrella*, a symbol of protection (the Bhattis trace their descent from Krishna), on top of Meghadamber, Cloud Tower.

The fort's rather drab main square, *Satiyon ki Sidhiyan*, is partly enclosed by magnificently carved sandstone palaces known as the **Raj Mahal** (these royal apartments are closed to the public). Here the women would perform their ritual sati on their husbands' pyres and this was also the site for the johars. The rawals would hold audience in Satiyon ki Sidhiyan from the white marble throne up the flight of steps. Below is Jessul's well where Lord Krishna struck the earth to bring forth fresh water and nearby is one of the fort's Hindu temples. An alley leads from behind the throne to an old cannon sticking through the ramparts; there is a splendid panorama over Jaisalmer from this spot.

Funeral pyres

In the past the wealthy Jain merchants provided finance for the rawals and in return they were allowed to build their own **temples** in the fort. Between the 12th and 16th C they erected a cluster of exquisitely crafted shrines to their tirthankers which are like a dense warren of chambers and corridors with the ceilings, pillars and walls covered in beautifully carved nymphs, gladiators, musicians, Hindu gods and other revered idols. A

Jain library

Jain temple guide will explain the symbolism. Stored in a vault underneath the Sambhavnath temple is an old *library* with thousands of priceless Jain manuscripts, astrological charts and paintings, some dating from the 11th C. Once a 15-km tunnel ran from here to a similar subterranean treasure room in Lodurva.

People still live up in the fort and there are a few small hotels built in the thick walls—most notable is the Jaisal Castle.

Havelis and Palaces in Jaisalmer

The merchants built their homes, their havelis, in the shadow of the fort, Havelis rise three to six storeys and enclose a small courtyard (*haveli* means a closed space in Persian). The inhabitants looked inward, prefering to live their lives unexposed to the streets and hence windows, doors and balconies overlook this inner yard and there is a well

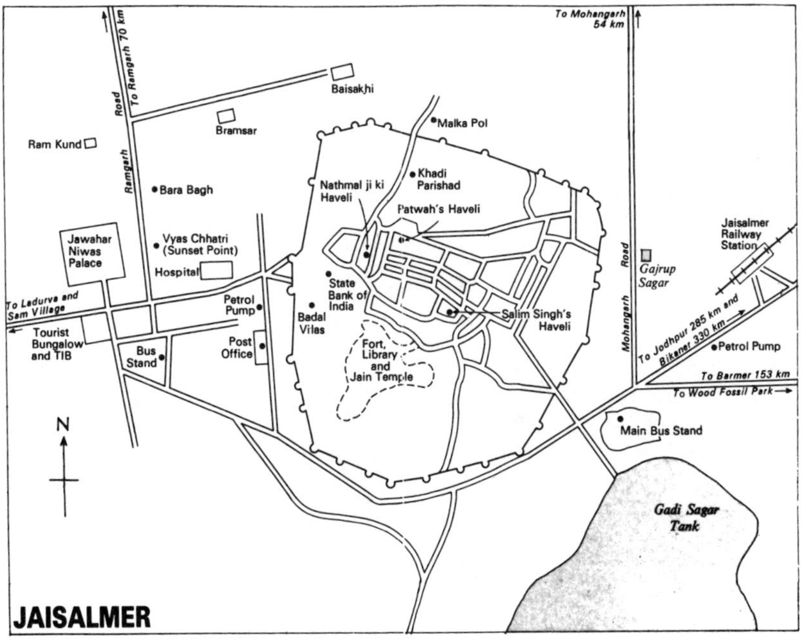

The Salim Singh ki Haveli at Jaisalmer

here, so the house has its own water supply. The **Salim Singh ki Haveli** is an extraordinary building with its top floor enclosed by a finely carved protruding balcony, thus giving it a top-heavy appearance. Once the house had two additional storeys, but the rawal did not like the idea of his subjects displaying such grandeur and ordered them to be dismantled.

The 'vampire' of Jaisalmer

Salim Singh Mohta, the man who had this haveli built as his family home, was Jaisalmer's prime minister in the early 1800s. He was notorious for his cruelty: 'Though the tenents of his faith (the Jain) imperatively prescribe the necessity of "hurting no senient being", and of sitting in the dark rather than, by luring a moth into the flame of a lamp, incure the penalty attached to the sin of insect-murder, this man has sent more of the sons of Jessoh (Jaisalmer) to Yamaloca (Pluto's realm) than the sword of their external foes during his long administration . . . Assuredly he is never mentioned, either in poetry or prose, but as a vampire draining the lifeblood of a whole people' (Tod). By introducing exhorbitant taxes Salim Singh Mohta forced many people into exile—some villages still lie deserted as a result of this migration—and through extortion he amassed great wealth for himself. Salim died in the 1820s and his descendants now live in Hyderabad. People live in part of his haveli; nevertheless visitors are welcome.

Larger and even more ornate is the **Patwon ki Haveli**, once home of the Patwa family who traded in gold, silver and opium. The delicate latticework has been beautifully carved and it took from 1800 to 1850 to complete the construction. The haveli is down a narrow gloomy alley and most of it lies empty, though it is open to visitors between 10.30 and 17.00. There are some fine murals in one of the rooms.

The most recent of the great havelis is the **Nathmaliji ki Haveli**, built for Nathmaliji, prime minister in the 1880s. The facade has been magnificently carved—'not even the white marble screen in the

Taj Mahal or anything at Fatehpur Sikri can compare with the stone carvings of Nathmaliji ki Haveli', boasts a local guide book—and was the work of two Moslem brothers. One worked on the left hand side, while the other worked on the right hand side and though the sides look symmetrical they are different and the details are never repeated. The large crack down the wall was caused by lightning. The house is occupied, but can be visited.

One of the best of the other buildings so skilfully carved out of sandstone is the **Badal Vilas**, the new palace, which was built free of cost as a gift from the local Moslem craftsmen. Nowadays it is the residence of the royal family and is not open to the public. The rawals' guests used to stay at the Jawahar Niwas, the fairly grand mansion outside the city walls opposite the Tourist Bungalow; it is now a seasonal hotel.

During its heyday Jaisalmer earned a fair proportion of its income through taxing passing caravans. It also had its own large market where merchants from the middle east, Afghanistan and other parts of India traded their wares. **Manak Chowk**, the site of this old market in the centre of the walled city, is still the main market though the merchandise today—food goods and domestic utensils—are not as exotic as they were in the past.

The courtesan and Krishna

A few minutes walk south of the city walls is **Gadi Sagar**, a tank built by Rawal Garsi in 1367 and for centuries Jaisalmer's sole source of water. Ghats, pavilions and temples, all made out of the characteristic golden sandstone, bank onto one section of the lake. The main route to the water's edge is through an attractive archway which was built as a home by Teelon, a celebrated courtesan. The rawal of the day gave orders that it should be pulled down, for he thought it improper that he and his family should have to walk under the archway inhabited by a sullied women every time they went to the lake. On hearing the news, Teelon hurriedly put a statue of Krishna in her room, thus making it a shrine, and the rawal, unable to knock down the archway-home cum shrine, was obliged to follow a different path to the water. In the early morning and evening women still come to collect water at Gadi Sagar.

View of the desert city

Around the other side of Jaisalmer, on a plateau a few kilometres northwest of the city, are the **royal cenotaphs**. From here you have a good view of Jaisalmer as a neat contained walled city rising from the flat desert. The scene is particularly evocative at sunset when the sun's last rays add an extra glow to the golden sandstone city. A camel trail in the foreground gives the picture a further romantic dimension.

Camel Treks and Other Excursions

Camel excursions, or safaris, into the surrounding desert have become increasingly popular with tourists in recent years. There are several organisations which are easily located in Jaisalmer (you can ask at the Tourist Office) which offer tailor-made trips for groups or individuals. The Narayan Hotel's safaris are well established.

Most popular is the four-day, three-night round trip to Mool Sagar and on to the Sam dunes and then back via Lodruvah and Amar Sagar. Alternatively there is the longer seven-day expedition to Pokaran or 11 days to Bikaner. A day's outing to Lodruvah is also possible.

As yet there are no luxurious upmarket safaris. Most typically you are given a camel, a local camel man (who is likely to know at least a smattering of English) and a cook. Food, usually rice, chapattis, dhal and vegetable curry, is included in the price of the trip, as is the use of blankets—and a tent if you do not want to sleep out in the open. The best time to come is between October and February when the weather is most favourable. There are also jeep safaris.

There are villages—some lie abandoned, deserted after Jaisalmer's decline in the last century—and patches of cultivated land which are like oases amidst the scrub vegetation of the arid western Thar.

Bada Bagh, a short distance beyond the royal cenotaphs, has a pretty cluster of orchards and it serves as a small market garden providing fruit and vegetables for Jaisalmer; an old dam contains the water which is channelled for the irrigation of the fields. Bada Bagh was developed as a pleasure garden for the rawals as far back as the 16th C.

About 5 km northwest of Jaisalmer are the lovely formal gardens of **Amar Sagar** which were created in the 1740s. They lay neglected until recently and now the ruined Jain temple is undergoing renovation and the gardens are receiving their fair share of care.

Continuing along the same road you reach **Lodurvah**, 15 km out of Jaisalmer. Once a magnificent city, it was the Bhattis' capital before Jaisal founded Jaisalmer in the 12th C. Temples and palaces, many decorated with beautiful carvings, were left to deteriorate, though fortunately some have been saved from total collapse by an impressive restoration programme.

Tale of love and death

There is a favourite tale which the guide in Lodruva is fond of relating. The beautiful Princess Moomal lived at the Moomal ki Mehri. Many an eligible prince asked for her hand in marriage, but she politely rebuffed their advances preferring a clandestine love affair with Prince Mahendra of Amarkot. On one occasion Mahendra arrived late only to find Moomal asleep beside someone else. He left heartbroken. Moomal's bed companion had been her sister, who, eager to see what Mahendra was like, had disguised herself as a minstrel of the chamber. However the two princesses had fallen asleep while waiting for their prince. Desperate to put the record straight, Moomal disguised herself and went in search of Mahendra and when she eventually found him tears welled in his eyes—though he did not recognise her. She asked why he was sad, to which he replied that a birthmark on her hand reminded him of a lover lost to another person. Moomal could restrain herself no longer; she revealed her identity and the two of them embraced, but their love for each other was so great that their bodies stopped functioning and the couple died in each other's arms.

9 km west of Jaisalmer you pass by **Mool Sagar**, another attractive oasis garden, which was a popular retreat for Rawal Mool Raj II at the beginning of the last century; he built a country palace for himself here.

A further 30 km or so down the same road and you reach the **Sam**, where the Thar desert finally turns into Sahara-like rolling sand dunes. There is nothing here, though tourists are brought to Sam to see the sandscape and there are plans to build simple dhanis (huts) for accommodation. It is a memorable experience sleeping out in the desert—the night is crisp and chilly, the skies are clear, the stars spangle and at full moon there is a marvellous tinge of electric light in the air. Festivals and shows are sometimes held at Sam.

A night in the desert

South of Sam is the huge **Desert National Park** covering 3162 sq km in the heart of the Thar Desert. The park is a sanctuary for endangered species of desert fauna and flora, some unique to this part of India, and there are programmes to protect the vegetation from the overgrazing and soil erosion which it has suffered in the past. Those wishing to visit the park require special permission from Jaisalmer. More accessible is the **Akal Wood Fossil Park** on the road to Barmer where the tree fossils date back 180 million years.

PRACTICAL INFORMATION

JAISALMER

Anyone making the effort to go to Jaisalmer stays there at least a day or two: you do not just pass through.

There is no palace hotel in Jaisalmer; the old palace is still occupied by the ex-royal family. However, the palatial style sandstone *Jhavan Niwas* (tel: 9; mid- to upper range price bracket), out on the west side of the city, was once the guest house for British VIPs and now serves as a small 'part time' hotel (usually only the high season). Opposite, and also attractively fashioned in sandstone, is the more modern *Moomal Tourist Bungalow* (tel: 92; mid-range price bracket). Both hotels are about five minutes walk from the western gate of the city walls.

In the northern quarter of the walled city you will find the *Narayan Niwas Hotel* (tel: 108; upper range price bracket), formerly a caravanserai for travelling merchants and their camels. The building encloses a large courtyard; the rooms are simple, though pleasant and with basic mod cons (overpriced for what they are). It is generally regarded as the best hotel in town.

But more interesting is the *Jaisal Castle* (tel: 62; lower to mid-range price bracket), a fascinating old house partially built into the western wall of the citadel itself. The dozen or so pokey rooms are simply furnished with traditional pieces; the views to the west at sunset are wonderful.

A crop of small **basic lodges**, invariably of the lower range price bracket, have grown up in the past few years and are flourishing in response to the increase in backpackers visiting Jaisalmer. They can be found within and outside the city walls.

There is basic accommodation enroute to Jaisalmer at the road junctions of Pokaran and Phalodi and to the south at Barmer.

MOUNT ABU

Not surprisingly, myth claims that Rajputs were created at Mount Abu, the highest, loveliest, most celestial place in Rajasthan. This was never a bloodstained battlefield like so many other tracts of Rajasthan—quite the contrary, Mount Abu was where Rajput maharajas built pleasure palaces. And they would escape up here, to their secular paradise, when the summer plains became a blistering hell.

The Holy Mountain

The Rajput's origins are shrouded in mythology and the Agnicula (Fire Born) clans claim they were born on Mount Abu.

Brahmins once ruled this part of India, but as they were not strong enough to ward off the demons they turned to the holy men to generate a warrior race.

Birth of the warrior race

The holy men returned to their retreat at Mount Abu, records a text of local folklore, 'with Indra, Brimha, Roodra, Vishnu, and all the inferior divinities, in their train. The fire-fountain anhulcoond was lustred with the waters of the Ganges; expiatory rites were performed, and, after a protracted debate, it was resolved that Indra should initiate the work of re-creation. Having formed an image (pootli) of the dhuba grass, he sprinkled it with the water of life, and threw it into the fire-fountain. Thence, on pronouncing the sajivan mantri (incantation to give life), a figure slowly emerged from the flame, bearing in the right hand a mace and exclaiming "Mar! Mar!"—"Slay! Slay!"'. After the new-born warriors had been created they fought a bloody battle against the demons and 'when the Dytes (demons) were slain, shouts of joy rent the sky; ambrosial showers were shed from heaven; and the gods drove their cars (vahan) about the firmament, exulting at the victory thus achieved. Of all the thirty-six royal races (says Chund, the

A holy man of Rajasthan

Panorama from Mount Abu

great bard of the Chohans), the Agnicula are the greatest: the rest were born of women.'

The Chauhans, who were one of the four Agnicula clans, ruled the kingdom of Sirohi in which Mount Abu was the most important place. In the mid-15th C they lost it to Rana Kumbha of Mewar who constructed one of his many forts on top of one of the hills. It would appear that Mount Abu was too off the beaten track to interest the Mughals and, indeed, the annals of Mount Abu are not coloured with glorious tales of heroism as at other strongholds in Rajasthan. Rather, Mount Abu is famous as a holy retreat and as Rajasthan's only hill station, a lovely cool lush refuge from the summer's scorching plains.

Ascending Mount Abu

From **Abu Road** (which is the name of a town) a road winds its way up the thickly wooded slopes to Mount Abu, the son of the Himalayas according to mythology, and the highest point in the Aravalli

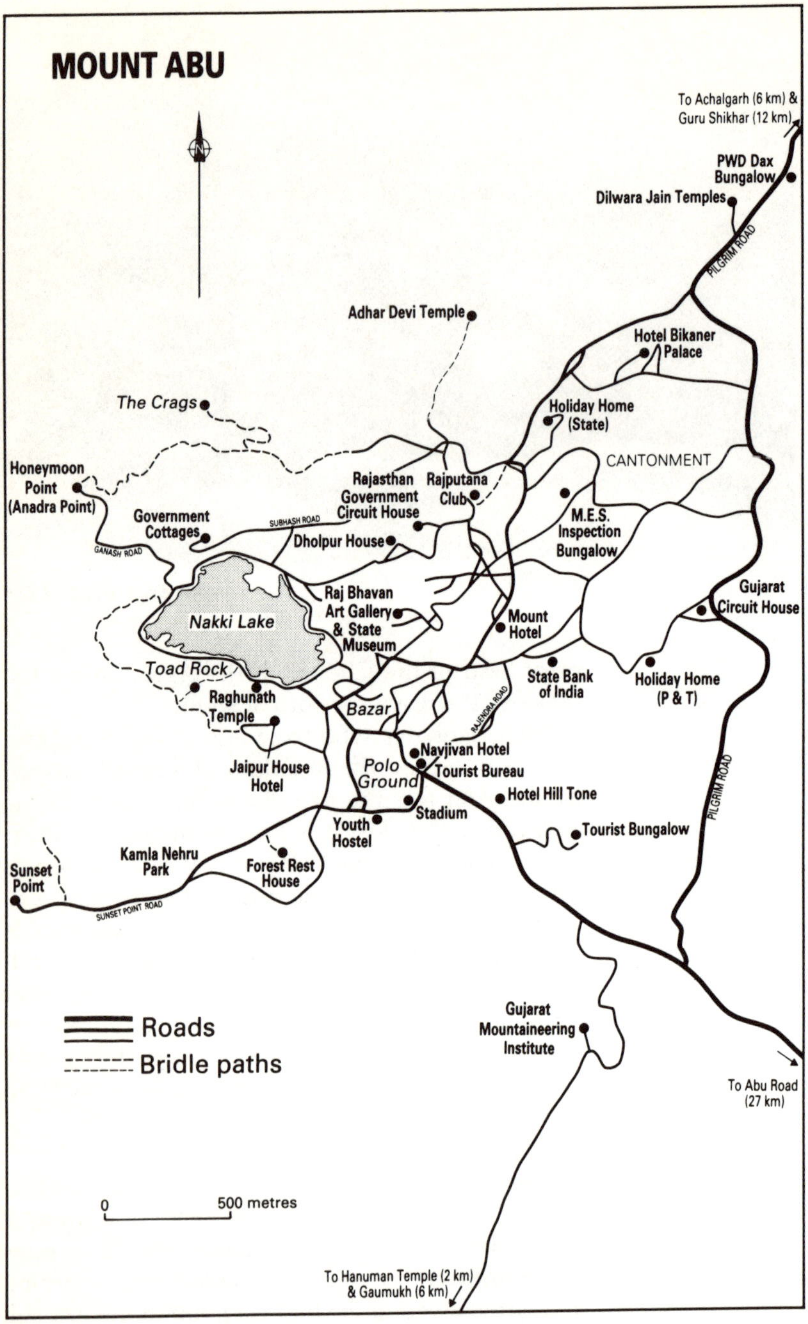
MOUNT ABU
To Achalgarh (6 km) & Guru Shikhar (12 km)
PWD Dax Bungalow
Dilwara Jain Temples
PILGRIM ROAD
Adhar Devi Temple
Hotel Bikaner Palace
The Crags
Holiday Home (State)
CANTONMENT
Honeymoon Point (Anadra Point)
Rajasthan Government Circuit House
Rajputana Club
Government Cottages
SUBHASH ROAD
Dholpur House
M.E.S. Inspection Bungalow
GANASH ROAD
Raj Bhavan Art Gallery & State Museum
Gujarat Circuit House
Nakki Lake
Mount Hotel
Toad Rock
State Bank of India
Holiday Home (P & T)
Raghunath Temple
Bazar
RAJENDRA ROAD
Jaipur House Hotel
Navjivan Hotel
Polo Ground
Tourist Bureau
Hotel Hill Tone
Stadium
PILGRIM ROAD
Youth Hostel
Tourist Bungalow
Kamla Nehru Park
Sunset Point
Forest Rest House
SUNSET POINT ROAD
Roads
Bridle paths
Gujarat Mountaineering Institute
To Abu Road (27 km)
0
500 metres
To Hanuman Temple (2 km) & Gaumukh (6 km)

range (1722 metres at Gurushikar). The name Abu is derived from Arbuda the serpent which rescued Nandi, Shiva's bull, when it fell into a gorge.

A path, branching to the left just before you reach Mount Abu town (see below) leads to the **Gaumukh temple** (after 5 km you reach a flight of 700 steps), so called because a spring flows through the mouth of a marble sculpted cow. This was the spot where the holy men created the Agnicula clans and nearby there is an image of Nandi, who was rescued by Arbuda, and also a shrine to Arbuda.

Pushing north out of town another track leads off the main road to the bottom of a flight of 200 steps. It is a steep climb up the side of the hill to the small **Adhar Devi temple** which has been chiselled out of a rock. The shrine is the oldest on Mount Abu.

The Olympus of the Hindus

Continue along the main road and about 3 km north of town you will reach the Dilwara Jain temples. Tod described Mount Abu as the 'Olympus of the Hindus' and none of any of the gods' houses up here are as splendid as at **Dilwara**. These white marble temples are amongst the finest and most skilfully crafted you will find anywhere in India.

Two temples are of special note. Started in 1031 the **Vimal Vasahi temple**, named after Vimal, a prosperous merchant and minister under the powerful Rajput ruler Bhim Deva, is dedicated to Adinath, the first Jain tirthankar. Local folklore boasts that it took 1500 sculptors and 1400 labourers 14 years to build the temple. A procession of white marble elephants leads up to the entrance and, though the temple does not look anything that special from the outside, once inside you are overwhelmed by the profusion of detailed carving. There are sections which have been chiselled in the minutest detail from the base of the pillars to the top of the domes; each piece of carving has some symbolic reference. Vimal and his family have been cut out of marble and are represented sitting on elephants and in the central shrine of the inner sanctum is the cross-legged figure of Adinath. In the surrounding cloisters there are 52 niches each with an identical statue of a tirthankar. The most exceptional portion of work is the exquisitely carved domed ceiling.

Neminath temple was built later, in 1230, by two brothers, Tejpala and Vasupala, and is dedicated to Neminath, the twenty-second tirthankar. Once again everything is intricately carved. Most delicate of all is the remarkable lotus flower which hangs like a pendant from the centre of a dome and so finely has it been crafted that it appears almost transparent. Business for the Jain merchants, the patrons of the temples, was flourishing at the time and, according to legend, they paid their artisans gold and silver in weights comparable to the weight of the marble they carved.

The temple opening times for non-Jains are from 12.00 to 18.00. There is a small camera charge if you want to take photos. No leather whatsoever is permitted inside the temples.

A couple of kilometres beyond is **Trevor's tank**, a small lake built by a British engineer in a wooded area. Once a favourite hunting spot of the maharajas it is now a popular patch with bird watchers.

Just off the main road 10 km from Mount Abu town you come to **Mandakini kund**, a tank overlooked by carved water buffaloes. They represent the demons which once disguised themselves as these sacred animals and used to come every night to gorge themselves on the ghee which filled the tank. One night the king killed them. The nearby **Shiva temple** has a greatly revered brass statue of Nandi, a toe of Shiva and a hole—where Shiva's lingam once was—which passes directly to the centre of the earth. The path up the hill leads to the remains of **Achalgarh**, Rana Kumbha's fort which was constructed on an earlier 10th C fort. Those who do not fancy the slog up to the top hire porters to carry them in the local equivalent of a sedan chair.

Finally, 15 km out of Mount Abu town, the road

The highest point in Rajasthan

reaches **Gurushikar**, the highest point in Rajasthan. There is the small **Atri Rishi temple** at the summit and a bell dating from the 15th C. On the neighbouring hill you can see the government research centre. Below, the foothills unfold into the plains of Rajasthan, and there are a couple of juice bars perched up here for those who want to rest awhile and take in the vast panorama.

Mount Abu Town

Juice bars are one of the most popular attractions back in **Mount Abu town**, long a favoured hill retreat with Indians during the hot summer months. Maharajas would pass part of the season up here with their families and take in a bit of tiger shooting; now it swarms with more humble folk and a saunter down to the juice bar ice cream parlours by Nakki Lake seems to be the thing to do.

There is a real holiday atmosphere up at Mount Abu during the summer. Many Gujarati families flee here from the sweltering heat back home and,

Nakki Lake, created by the gods

as an added bonus to the party mood, alcohol is available in Rajasthan whereas it is not in dry Gujarat. Honeymooning couples walk hand in hand, something they are less likely to do in their more conservative home environments.

The focal point of Mount Abu town is the lovely **Nakki Lake** which was dug out by the gods with their nails (nakhs) and around the lake there are various temples, the most important one being the old **Shri Raghunathji Hindu temple** on the south side.

Lovers' walks. . .

For many, a stroll around Nakki is a pleasant evening recreation, or you can take a boat out into the lake. Keep an eye out for **Toad Rock,** a large rock on the south side which looks like a toad about to leap; other look-alike rocks require a keener imagination if you are to detect their alleged resemblence. Walk beyond Nakki down Ganesh Road and you will come to **Honeymoon Point** where there are fabulous views out over the flat plains, especially spectacular at sunset. There are various other viewpoints nearby and an annual festival is held at the Ganesh temple here during the rainy season. Alternatively take another route out of town and you come to popular **Sunset Point**, which, as the name implies, is a good vantage for watching the sunset. On the other side of town there is **Sunrise Point** looking out to the east.

and spiritual enlightenment

Near to the Nakki Lake you will come across the **World University of Spiritual Knowledge and Raja Yoga Training**, the headquarters of the Brahma Kumaris and one of the most recent additions to the 'Olympus of the Hindus'. The large white palatial building is at the top of a long wide flight of steps. Corridors lead from the entrance hall to meditation, yoga and prayer rooms. Everywhere is clean and brilliantly lit by neon lights and on the walls there are gaudy, brightly coloured models and paintings of saints and scenes from the 'Golden Age'. The Brahma Kumari sect was created in 1937 by the 'Incorporeal Supreme Father Knowledgeful God Shiva (through Corporeal Medium of Prajapita

Brahma)' and in their introductory booklet they outline their aims and objectives thus:

Aims:

1) To teach Raja Yoga in order to eradicate vices, viz, sex-lust, anger, avarice, attachment, arrogance, jealousy, lethargy, etc, and thus remove tension while performing normal duties of life in a peaceful way.

2) To impart spiritual knowledge in order to make man's intellect divine for re-establishing the Golden Age of complete purity, peace and prosperity in Bharat in particular and the world in general.

Objectives:

1) To create deeper awareness of the important role of spirituality in human development.

2) To understand our ties and responsibilities in society and work together to achieve reconciliation, human values and peace.

3) To introduce a practical programme everywhere emphasising the importance of world brotherhood (being children of one God, the world Father) and thus maintain global equilibrium.

The Brahma Kumaris have 750 centres, including 85 Spiritual Museums, worldwide. The Spiritual Museum at Mount Abu is between the Polo Ground and Nakki Lake. You can attend courses (you do not have to be a signed-up member of the sect) including a 'Three-day Raja Yoga camp', 'Seven-day self-realisation and godly knowledge course' and the even longer 'Life time course'.

It is easy enough to find buses and jeeps to take you back down the 27 km to Abu Road, Mount Abu's road and railway link to the rest of Rajasthan.

PRACTICAL INFORMATION

MOUNT ABU

The accommodation situation at Mount Abu is different to elsewhere in Rajasthan. Being a hill station and a holiday resort it gets inundated with (Indian) tourists during the summer months, when the hotels and the self-contained cottages (which cater primarily for families and couples) are in great demand. To evoke the spirit of good times and glamour some hoteliers have decorated their honeymoon suites like sets from favourite Hindi movies and even a few of the hotel names, such as 'Hilltone', imbue a touch of chicness. Accommodation rates are higher during the summer season.

Some maharajas from around Rajasthan had summer palaces at Mount Abu. Only that of Bikaner's is still in a fair state of repair and it is now a hotel. The *Palace Hotel* (tel: 21; upper range price bracket; 28 rooms) lies in lovely wooded seclusion near to the Dilwara Temples, blissfully apart from all the action in downtown Mount Abu. As with other Bikaner residences, the Palace Hotel has not undergone lavish conversions, but it is a charming hotel and the old furnishings and laid back atmosphere remain dusty, though intact.

In town, the *Abu International* (tel: 177) by the polo ground and the *Hotel Hilltone* (tel: 137) near the bus stand are two of the better, modern upper range price bracket hotels.

The *Shikar Tourist Bungalow* (tel: 29; mid-range price bracket) near the petrol station has an attractive setting on the edge of town, as has the *Circuit House* (tel: 25), out of town and off the road to Dilwara.

Lower to mid-range price bracket accommodation in Mount Abu town includes: the *Arawali* (tel: 216), the *Bharti* (tel: 61), the *Navjivan* (tel: 73) and its annexe the *Samrat* (tel: 73).

INDEX

NOTES

NOTES